ORCHID CULTURE

IN CEYLON AND THE EAST

ORCHID CULTURE

IN CEYLON AND THE EAST

F. A. E. PRICE

GYAN

Published by

GYAN

Gyan Publishing House
5, Ansari Road
Daryaganj, New Delhi-110002
Phone: 011-47034999, 9811692060
E-mail: books@gyanbooks.com

Distribution Network
gyanbooks.com
India, USA, Canada, UK, Australia, France

ISBN : 978-81-212-3851-9 (PB)
First Published, Colombo, 1918

2nd Impression 2020

Printed at: Gyan Press, Delhi.

Orchid Culture in Ceylon and the East
Author: F. A. E. Price

ORCHID CULTURE
IN CEYLON AND THE EAST

by F. A. E. PRICE, J.P.
PRESIDENT OF THE CEYLON ORCHID SOCIETY

THE COLOMBO APOTHECARIES
COMPANY LIMITED
PRINTERS PUBLISHERS AND BOOKSELLERS

ONCIDIUM PAPILIO MAJUS
(Trinidad).

FOREWORD TO FIRST EDITION

The author of this little volume is to be congratulated on his energy and initiative. *Orchid Culture* is doubtless the first book published in Ceylon, if not in tropical Asia, exclusively devoted to orchids. What is equally creditable, especially in these times, is that it is entirely a labour of love. There are a good many orchid enthusiasts in Ceylon, but it is only natural that it should remain for a Planter to write a book on a subject of culture.

The cult of the orchid has long had a peculiar fascination, and the possession of an orchid collection has been regarded as the hall-mark of respectability and affluence. Probably no other family of the vegetable kingdom is surrounded with so much romance. One well-known orchid firm in England not long ago employed experienced travellers to explore the tropics, especially of America and Asia, for rare orchids, chartered ships for transporting them to England, and built a railway station adjoining spacious hot houses where special trains unloaded their precious cargo. It may not be easily credited in a country where orchids of one sort or another are found almost on every tree, that as much has been paid for a single orchid as would purchase a good-sized estate in Ceylon. Not long ago a reward of £2,000 was offered and paid by the well-known firm of Messrs. Sander & Sons, Herts, for the re-discovery of *Cypripedium Fairieanum* in Assam.

In the tropics orchid-growing is capable of affording infinite pleasure, and need not by any means be regarded as the hobby of millionaires. Here in fact they often thrive better "on air," as on tree trunks, than otherwise. We only require a Joseph Chamberlain here to make the orchid button-hole as popular as the rose. But I must not anticipate the good things which the following pages contain.

1918 H. F. MACMILLAN.

FOREWORD TO FIRST EDITION

PREFACE TO FIRST EDITION

It is with much trepidation that I write a short guide to the culture, in Ceylon and the East, of some of the better known orchids; in fact my only reason for so doing is that I am told by a well known Ceylon Horticulturist that such a guide, free from technicalities, would be of interest, and perhaps of use, to the very keen growers of these lovely plants, and there are many of them in Ceylon and India; and if it proves of any interest or use to these, it will have achieved its object.

I am no Botanist so cannot pretend to any technical or botanical terms, therefore propose to give a few simple cultural directions which should enable anyone to grow orchids to perfection with a little care and management. (It should be clearly understood, however, that this little book does not cater for experienced growers nor yet for Botanists).

However careful and minute these directions may be, it is, of course, in the grower's hands that success or failure lies, and careful observations of the plants as regards shading, watering, etc. will be of far more value as time goes on than the very fullest instructions.

My authorities on a few points are *Orchids*, by Watson and Chapman, Macmillan's *Handbook*, and *Orchids for Everyone*, by Curtis.

The illustrations are from paintings I have made from flowers in my collection or from photographs of these. It is, of course, impossible to reproduce the natural colours of the flowers, but the coloured plates in this book reflect great credit and show much care and trouble taken on the part of the Printers.

F. A. E. PRICE.

Neuchâtel, Neboda.
October 30th, 1918.

PREFACE TO SECOND EDITION

In response to many requests—extended over equally many years—for copies of my little book of orchids, (requests which by the way I have been unable to meet owing to the first edition being sold out) I venture once more to place it before the ' orchid-minded ' public. It goes out with the sole idea of extending the cult of the orchid and the assurance that all of us—rich and poor alike (and who is rich these days !) can grow at least a few of these lovely plants. Since 1918—when the first edition saw light, or Printer's ink—much water has flowed under the various bridges which lead the way to orchid culture, prices have come down, knowledge has grown and, above all, the fact that orchids are in themselves, lovely, have awakened a desire in almost everyone to grow at least one or two plants.

Poor things ! (the orchids I mean !)—they are very often killed by over-kindness; imported plants, eagerly awaited, valiantly bloom once and then gradually degenerate into "weedy" specimens and are eventually discarded as useless.

And how utterly unnecessary ! There is, I am glad to say, a new spirit abroad to-day ; no longer are the epiphytal orchids treated as cannas or caladiums and potted in heavy soil and allowed to bloom and die.' No, they are treated *as* orchids—very simply, very ordinarily—and yet they bloom regularly and frequently. No one would think of treating say paddy and coconuts in the same way, nor even tea and rubber—and yet that is what has been the case with orchids: no wonder they died ! Of my own experience I can safely say that I would sooner look after an ordinary amateur's collection of orchids than take over a fruit orchard—so easy are they to manage and grow ; and one is so aptly rewarded for the very little care required; and moreover the initial cost is now so very reasonable.

At one time one was looked upon as a Croesus or ' Joseph Chamberlain ' if one imported an orchid. *Now* you can see members of the great family at almost any resthouse in Ceylon ! and many of the very finest plants can be bought for the cost of an imported rose.

In the body of this little book—which has been completely revised and brought up to date, as far as possible—I have tried to analyse the cultural hints on the various species; but, and it is a big one, I have *not* included families from overseas which in my opinion, are of little or no horticultural value; for after all, it is flowers we want, not orchids of scientific or botanical interest; nor have I given long lists of hybrids between various families—such may be found in any dealer's trade catalogue, and no useful purpose would be served by my re-capitulating them. Rather have I devoted my attention to plants that will thrive with the least trouble and produce flowers that their owners can be (and will be) proud of. The only exceptions to this are to be found among the few indigenous and Eastern orchids which certainly deserve mention, if only because they are indigenous and Eastern.

The recently-formed Orchid Society of Ceylon will, I hope, go a long way towards popularising the cult of the orchid in Ceylon and the East in general, for we hope to establish 'exchange' relations with other kindred bodies and members who live in other countries, and as I have been honoured by being elected the first President of the Society, I cannot do less than wish it, its energetic Secretary and its members every possible success in its work and activities, and may it so spread the knowledge of the ease of orchid growing, that ere long we shall see at least one plant in every household or garden—as common (and as gorgeous) as a lovely canna or rose.

It is for these beginners that I once more launch this little book in the earnest hope that it will at least help them in some of their difficulties, to safeguard the money they have spent, and to extend the knowledge and love of orchids.

F. A. E. Price.

Elkaduwa Group,
Elkaduwa.
July, 1933

ILLUSTRATIONS

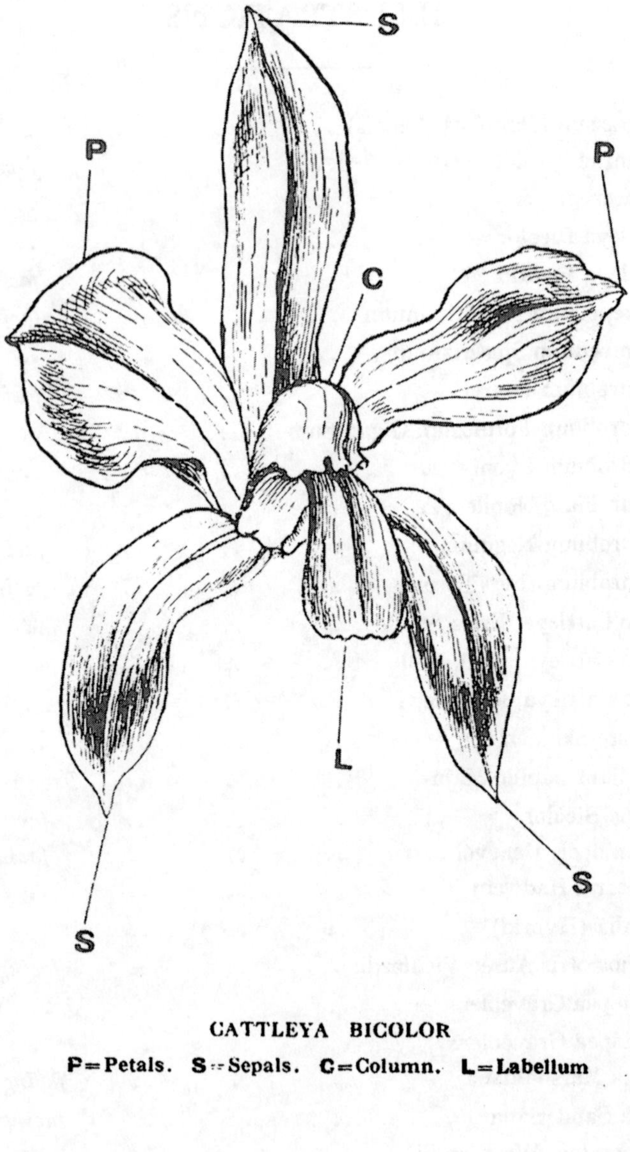

CATTLEYA BICOLOR

P=Petals. S=Sepals. C=Column. L=Labellum

ERRATUM

Page 13. Para 3. Line 6.

For *Lycaste Skinneri* read *Cattleya Bicolour.*

Page 117. Selection for Medium elevations: include *Zygopetalum.*

ORCHID CULTURE FOR BEGINNERS

Orchidaceæ.

The family *Orchidaceæ* contains many thousands of species and varieties, not to mention anything of the thousands of hybrids that have been raised artificially, but the flowers of all of them, though differing enormously in size, shape, coloration, habit, etc., are formed upon one common plan, which is, after all, but a modification of that which obtains in the common primrose, violet or geranium.

Structure of flowers.

The orchid is remarkable for the fact that the third petal, usually at the base of the flower, is almost always totally different from the other two petals. This third petal is known as the lip (or *labellum*) and is more often than not the great feature of the plant by reason of its sometimes extraordinary size, form, or coloration.

Another remarkable feature in the orchid is the "column." This takes the place of the stamens and pistils in other flowers, and which are, there, separate organs. In an orchid, however, they are as it were amalgamated into one central, often waxy-textured and club-shaped organ. An idea of the foregoing may be gathered from a study of the flower of *Lycaste Skinneri*, which is here drawn natural size, and in which the sepals, petals, labellum and column are clearly marked. As is well known, orchids fall naturally into two sections, i.e., terrestrial and epiphytic. Epiphytal orchids are those that are found naturally growing upon trees and branches or in crevices of rocks. It must, however, be remembered that an epiphyte is not a parasite, for a parasite is a plant, animal or micro-organism that obtains its nourishment from its "host" whereas an epiphyte uses its "host" merely as a support, and obtains its nourishment from the surrounding atmosphere. In addition to the foregoing, orchids show a remarkable range in regard to growth, habit and duration of the plants, stems, leaves, etc., some of them grow in large, dense tufts, while others have long creeping rhizomes from which the roots and pseudo-bulbs are produced: others again have rush-like foliage, in fact they may present an infinite variety of growth.

Pseudo-bulbs.

"Pseudo-bulb" is the name given to the stem-like growths that occur in most orchids, and may take the place of stems: they are not stems, neither are they bulbs nor leaf-stalks, but appear to take the place of all three. A pseudo-bulb may be swollen as in the *Cattleyas*, woody as in some of the *Dendrobiums*, flattened as in some of the *Coelogynes*; again they may not be present at all, as in the genera *Cyprepedium*, *Selenipedium*, *Satyrium*, etc.

Pseudo-bulbs are usually produced annually from the growing point, one each season, but in some cases several are produced and they are often persistent for as long as the plant is in existence, but this is not always the case for in some families they are of annual duration only (*Thunia* and allies).

They may be bare or leafy, and the flowers are borne from the sides, apices or bases of the mature pseudo-bulbs, while in the cases of the plants that do not produce pseudo-bulbs the flowers are usually borne on scapes from the centres of the plants.

Colour of Orchids.

There is a practically infinite range of colour to be found among orchids; purples, mauves and yellows being perhaps the commonest; blue is one of the scarcest of colours among them, but the lovely *Vanda cœrulea*, with its masses of large pale-blue flowers amply compensates for this deficiency.

Fragrance of Orchids.

Again, orchids appeal to many people on account of their fragrance; several of the *Cattleyas*, *Cœlogynes*, *Dendrobiums*, *Aerides*, *Vandas*, etc., being very highly scented; indeed it is very seldom that an orchid is neither fragrant nor malodorous, though the percentage of the latter is very small. (*Dendrobium superbum* being strongly scented with rhubarb and *Bulbophyllum Beccari* having a very fœtid odour).

Long-lasting.

Some of them are also exceptionally long-lasting when either cut for indoor use or left on the plant—two or more months being not at all uncommon. I have had *Dendrobium Dearei* and *Cyprepedium Spicerianum* in full flower for over ten weeks.

Houses.

At low and medium elevations excellent orchid houses may be made on any clear level site as follows :—Erect uprights of wood or iron about fourteen feet high to form a house of the required shape and size, these should be placed about six feet apart. Wire netting is then stretched and firmly fastened outside the whole thing, and bamboo tats are spread on top to break the force of the sun, rain and wind. Orchids, by the way, are not improved by exposure to strong winds, particularly sea breezes.

If the floor can be either paved or cemented, so much the better (though it is not absolutely necessary) for, in hot weather water must be thrown about freely to give the requisite steamy atmosphere. If a fountain can be introduced it will be a great addition, as well as providing the necessary moisture and water. Around the sides of the house suitable flowering creepers may be grown; these provide a good background for the orchids, and keep out the overstrong rays of the sun. Pots of orchids can then be placed on two or three tiers around the sides of the house, and hanging pots and baskets can be suspended at will.

If an orchid house is to be made, then it should be so constructed as to catch all the early morning sun, but just as good results may be obtained in a sunny verandah.

Orchids like sunlight, but not full exposure at the hottest part of the day. There are one or two exceptions only and they are dealt with under their own names, but it will be found that most orchids grow on trees or in a lightly shaded area where the sun's force is broken by foliage, etc.

Ceylon is, on the whole, but poorly represented by orchids of any size or beauty, though there are many species to be found, but these are mainly of botanical interest. An exception must of course be made for the lovely *Dendrobium Mc Carthiæ* (Wesak-Mal) which is endemic and only found near Ratnapura, *D. aureum*, *Vanda Rox burghii* and one or two more.

It is hard to say why this is so, as India has provided a large number of well-known and showy species; while Java, Burma and Malaya have given us some of the very best of known orchids.

In order to grow orchids successfully it is necessary to know whether the plants it is intended to grow are terrestrial or epiphytic, whether they are tropical or cool-climate species and also whether they require a rest after the growing season or not. Tropical orchids can, of course, be grown to perfection in the low-country, and also with great success at the higher elevations in glazed houses, provided that the latter are well ventilated, for orchids will not tolerate anything approaching stuffiness or stagnation in the atmosphere, though ventilation must not be carried to excess—nor do they like wet or cold feet.

During the growing season they enjoy liberal treatment in respect of water, warmth and light, and on very hot days they should be watered and syringed freely, care being taken that the foliage is dry before the cool evening temperature sets in and that water is not allowed to lodge in the young growths—if it does they may damp off and die, thus losing a season's flowers. When the flowers have faded and the leaves have fallen, most of them require a period of rest, with drier and cooler conditions, though some of them need water all the year round (but these are dealt with when described).

Potting, Composts, etc.

Orchids may be grown in pots, in wooden baskets, and in sections of giant bamboo; ordinary sunbaked roofing tiles, in which the plant and compost is held in and the whole suspended by a thin copper wire, are very useful.

Special pots may be procured locally and are cheap and effective. They should have plenty of drainage holes in the sides and bottom and may then be placed on the staging or suspended. Baskets should be made as permanent as possible and are well adapted for delicate species. An extra strip or two of wood nailed on to the bottoms will prevent the compost being washed out. They are easily made by any carpenter and are especially useful for some of the *Cœlogynes*, *Phalænopses* and *Dendrobiums*, etc. and merely consist of strips of hardwood, one inch wide by whatever length is required. Thin copper wire passed through the drilled ends will complete the job.

Whatever receptacle is used, care must be taken that it is quite clean and that it is not too large for the plant that is intended to occupy it, for most orchids (especially those that are epiphytes) prefer small pots and very little rooting material.

Before putting in the compost, plenty of clean, broken crocks must be put in to ensure good drainage. Very little compost is needed as a mass of this will hold the water and is liable to decompose, which would be fatal to the plants. When potting, the plants should be made firm in the compost, as they will root more freely than if left to sway about in the wind. As the plants are potted they should be labelled at once for future identification, and for this purpose, narrow pieces of zinc are very useful—the names being printed with an indelible pencil or ink.

A useful general compost for epiphytes may be composed of equal parts of finely broken crocks, fern or bracken roots cut into one inch lengths and shredded, a little moss, a few pieces of old bark and a little broken charcoal (the whole to be thoroughly mixed); while for terrestrial species it should contain (in addition to the above) some good fibrous loam, and a little clean sand and decomposed cow manure (and, if possible, some leaf mould). The ideal compost for orchids is a mixture of peat and sphagnum moss. I do not advocate the use of coir fibre.

Repotting of Established Plants.

This should only be done when the condition of the plants indicates the necessity, or when they have outgrown their pots, etc., and should never be done during the resting or growing season, but just prior to the commencement of the latter.

Orchids are greatly improved however if the surface material is replaced with fresh moss, etc., during the resting season, great care being taken that the roots are not injured in so doing. It is far better to break the pot (if necessary) than to injure the live roots of the plant. When repotting is done, all the old compost should be removed as well as the dead and decaying roots—which are far better if cut off. Very often the old compost may be syringed or washed out under a strong stream of water.

When potting is complete, water must be given sparingly and the plants should be shaded until new growth is observed, and, as these growths make progress, water and light may be given more liberally.

A most essential feature in potting orchids is the drainage, and to secure this quite one-third of the pot should be filled with clean, broken crocks over which is placed a thin layer of moss or broken charcoal.

Watering and Damping

Most orchids require plenty of water at the root and in the atmosphere during the growing season, the commencement of which is evidenced by the appearance of new pseudo-bulbs, production of leaves, and elongation of the roots in such genera as *Vanda, Aerides, Renanthera,* etc., while on hot, dry days spraying or syringing is very beneficial. I will interpolate a golden rule—*never* over water—most orchids are killed by over-kindness in this respect. When growth is complete, (i.e., when no further signs of activity are observed) they should be subjected to drier, airier and cooler conditions with a little more light; this is necessary in order to ripen and mature the new growths and to ensure their flowering. When the flower buds appear again however, they should be more liberally treated, but whilst in flower and for some time after flowering, very little water is needed. If water were given during the resting season, premature growths would be encouraged, to the great detriment of the plants, and these same growths would not bear flowers properly. Proper discretion is of course needed, and the plants should not be allowed to suffer at any time from severe drought. Rain water (or soft water) is essential for the successful cultivation of orchids, hard water being very liable to cause decomposition of the compost. If the plant *looks* healthy during the resting period—don't over water it.

Propagation.

Orchids may readily be increased from cuttings, division of the rootstock and from seed; the methods are as follows :—

Cuttings.—Most of the epiphytal orchids that produce long, deciduous-leaved pseudo-bulbs may be increased by cutting the older pseudo-bulbs into lengths of about four inches and placing them in a damp, warm and shaded position in well crocked pots of chopped moss and sand. They will soon produce roots and may then be potted up in the usual way, choosing small pots for the purpose. *Thunias, Arundinas* and other genera that do not produce proper pseudo-bulbs, may be increased by cuttings of the old stems being placed in pots of sand and treated in the same way.

Division of Rootstock.—This is an easy and fairly certain way of increasing orchids, and the procedure is obvious.

Seeds.—Orchids may be readily raised from seed, but as the long time it takes to ripen weakens the plant, and the length of time that elapses before the young seedlings may be reasonably expected to flower is so great, while the minuteness of the seed makes its germination and subsequent existence so precarious, most people are inclined to leave this kind of propagation to others!

But when it is considered that some hybrid orchids have fetched quite fabulous prices, it may perhaps be worth while to attempt some cross fertilization.

This is done by removing some of the pollen with a fine brush and placing it on the inside of the column (which has a viscid surface on the under side) of another flower, care being taken to note the parent's names for future reference.

After pollination the plants should be given every inducement to ripen good seed and should not be stinted as regards air, light and water. Usually the longer the seed takes to ripen, the more fertile it will be. When the seed is quite ripe it may be gently shaken out on to a saturated brick, which is standing with its base in warm water, and the whole should be placed in a warm position away from draughts and rain. The lightest current of air is sufficient to carry away the seed, so subsequent waterings will have to be made with the very finest of sprays.

A good method of watering is that of placing the seed bed in a shallow pan of warm rain-water. This soon percolates and moistens the surface (the surface of the seed-bed must not, however, be brought into direct contact with the water). When the seedlings have produced their roots and first leaves they should be potted up in minute pots in a fine, porous compost and given a warm, lightly-shaded position and encouraged to grow freely. There are other methods of sowing the seed, i.e., on calico squares, pieces of sawn timber, etc. (all of which are to be kept moist), but the conditions required are similar and the same treatment must be given.

The pollen masses will usually be found at the apices of the column, protected by little caps.

Since I wrote the foregoing notes on the cross-fertilization of orchids, I have discovered that one or two keen members of the Ceylon Orchid Society have given the matter careful thought and have actually raised some hybrid plants by the asymbiotic method; in which the seed is shaken into a sterilized flask containing a suitable rooting medium, which is of course, also sterilized and has been allowed to absorb the young seedlings' requirements in the way of chemical foods. This opens up a vast project, for it is usually found that hybrid orchids are hardier and more easily managed than their parents, while the crosses are often exceedingly beautiful. It is quite without the scope of this book to go into this matter in detail, but some very interesting and helpful literature has been prepared on the subject, particularly in the British West Indies, and would-be hybridisers are recommended to apply to the Honorary Secretary of the Club for further information on this absorbing subject.

It is as well to note that the formation of seed-pods and ripening of seed imposes rather a strain on the parent plants, so perhaps it would be best to start in on well-established and healthy parents for the purpose rather than risk young or rare plants until the hybridiser is sure of his ground.

NOW HERE ARE A FEW "DON'TS"

Don't pot up terrestrial and epiphytal orchids in the same compost or manner. Find out what your plants are and treat them accordingly. Epiphytes won't flourish in soil, nor ground orchids if tied on to trees.

Don't use more compost for epiphytes than is absolutely necessary.

Don't forget that epiphytes *must* be very well drained and that *no* orchid will thrive if its roots are permanently cold and wet.

Don't omit to finish potting up your epiphytes so that they "sit," as it were, on a slight mound, a little above the pot level. Terrestrial orchids may be finished off so that the soil is about half an inch below the rim of the pot.

Don't forget that *all* orchids like to be fairly firmly set in their rooting medium. They will start away better than if loose: but *don't* interpret this to mean that the compost must be rammed home!

Don't treat newly-imported orchids as if they were in full growth, *they are not*, and will probably die unless you treat them carefully. They will arrive brown and withered. Wash them carefully in tepid water, cut off all dead pseudo-bulbs and leaves and destroy any insects there may be. Then hang them up in the shade, head downwards on a string for a week or so, keeping them just damp.

When you see roots or new shoots appear, then is the time to pot them up, and *not until then.*

Don't hesitate to examine your compost, pots and plants, if you suspect that the former is going sour. If it is, and the plants are not attended to, *they will die.* See that the compost is all quite porous and quite clean.

Cleanliness is an essential point in the successful culture of orchids.

Don't let any of your plants get scorched by direct sunlight—except those that grow out in the open—on trees or in beds—and don't expose them to cold draughts or drips.

Don't leave them to the tender mercies of the garden cooly altogether; show him how to water them when they need it and then watch him. Now and again you will probably find that he just wets the leaves (awfully bad for the young growths) or he may try to keep them permanently sodden—(just as bad).

Don't put anything in your pots or baskets which will go sour or rot—orchids, like every other plant, like clean, wholesome surroundings; with plenty of aeration in the compost.

Don't keep them in a dark shady corner away from all sunlight.

Don't expect every species of orchid to flourish in the same manner in your locality, some will do better than others—concentrate on them. When you have gained considerable experience you can easily launch out into a bigger selection.

Don't lose sight of the fact that an orchid will *grow* if carelessly potted, it will *thrive* if you are careful over it, and gradually fill up with smaller stuff on top for the young roots to wander in.

Don't overdo the watering.

Don't be disheartened—they are *very* easy to cultivate if you treat them reasonably.

Don't forget that most orchid growers are only too glad to be able to give a helping hand in difficulties to their fellow growers, and will very likely be able to tell you just why you are not successful with any one particular plant.

Don't be ashamed of your modest collection ; like everything else, it will grow; and finally—

Don't hesitate to ask for advice

It may seem incredible, but during the last six months I have seen, in two different collections, the following amazing things. (Look them up later on, and then you will see that some "don'ts" are really necessary!). Number one grower had an imported *dendrobe* potted up in heavy loam! He said he "*knew all orchids grew on trees* (italics are mine) but he hadn't got any decent trees handy so did *the best he could* for them"! Number two had got a cutting of *arundina bambusifolia* tied to a tree in a coconut husk! Wild horses won't drag the names of these enthusiasts out of me!

SOME OF THE MORE WELL-KNOWN SPECIES IN ALPHABETICAL ORDER

As no hard and fast rules can be laid down for the culture of all orchids, for they differ so enormously, I propose to describe shortly some of them, giving, at the same time, a few simple hints on their management.

ACANTHOPHIPPIUM

A quaint genus of terrestrial orchids, natives of Asia. Pseudo-bulbs, one or two leaved, oblong, three inches high, pale green and fleshy, leaves ribbed, about eight inches long, oval and dull green. Flower scapes produced from the bases of the mature pseudo-bulbs, two- to three-flowered, flowers fairly large, tubular and of a waxy texture.

A. bicolor

Native of Ceylon (1500–3000 ft.), in heavy jungles under deep shade and occasionally in shady patnas, facing north as a rule. Flowers produced in summer on an erect three-flowered raceme, bright yellow, tipped with purplish red. May be grown in pots, in good loam. Should be kept shaded and given plenty of water in the growing season with a period of rest after the flowers have faded. This is a fairly common species.

Others are :—*A. Sylhetense, A. Striatum.*

ACRIOPSIS

A small family of epiphytal orchids from Java and Malaya ; well adapted for culture in baskets in a mixture of moss and broken charcoal. They require plenty of warmth and moisture in the growing season, and need not be rested to any extent.

A. Javanica

Pseudo-bulbs round, wrinkled and crowded, one inch in diameter bearing two apical and two lateral grassy, pointed leaves. Flower spike produced laterally in autumn, many-flowered.

ÆRIDES

A large family of tropical, epiphytal orchids, confined to Asia. They are strong-growing, free-flowering, handsome plants, and the leaves are usually strap-like, frequently bilobed at the apex. The flowers are often large, showy and fragrant.

Roots are produced freely from all parts of the stem, and it is useless to attempt to pot all of them. They may be grown in pots or baskets, and their potting is a simple matter :—After putting a good layer of broken crocks in the pot the plants should be placed in the centre with as many of the roots as possible, more crocks should then be pressed in with the roots, and the whole finished off with a layer of moss, this, with a good watering completes their requirements.

In subsequent pottings the decaying and dead roots should be cut off and clean moss should be put in to replace the old. They require a little more shading than their allies (*Saccolabiums, Vandas*, etc.) and may easily be grown on trees.

A. affine

(Synonymous with *A. multiflorum*, q.v.).

A. crassifolium

A very fine plant from Burma. Leaves thick and leathery, dull green, notched at the apex, eight inches long. Racemes axillary, semi-pendent, produced in early summer. Flowers large and fragrant, rosy-purple, the large labellum being trilobed and deep purple.

A. crispum

Native of India. Growth erect. Leaves much as in the foregoing. Racemes long and pendent, many-flowered, produced in summer. Flowers large and fragrant, white, flushed with pink.

A. Lawrenciæ

An exceptionally fine plant, native of the Philippine Islands. Stems and leaves much as in *A. virens* but larger and stiffer. The long, drooping raceme is borne in autumn and is many-flowered. The latter are large and fragrant and of a waxy consistence. Sepals and petals white, tinged with purple. Lip large and trilobed, the front lobe being deep purple while the side lobes are tinged with green. It is rather a scarce plant.

A. multiflorum

Leaves thick and fleshy, channelled, bilobed at the apex. Flowers small, rosy-mauve, sweet-scented, borne on a many-flowered drooping raceme in spring and summer. Native of Burma.

A. odoratum

This is about the best known *Aeride* and is a native of Burma and India. It is a handsome plant and the long strap-like leaves are leathery and channelled. The many-flowered raceme is produced in early summer. The latter are large, creamy-white and very fragrant. Sepals and petals tipped with purple.

A. quinquevulnerum

Native of the Philippines. Stems erect, clothed with two rows of long, strap-shaped leaves. Racemes axillary, produced in late summer, fourteen inches long, pendent and many-flowered. The flowers are large and showy and very fragrant. They are white, tipped with amethyst and blotched with five deep red blotches (hence the name). Spur, green.

A. vandarum

Ceylon and India, 4000 feet and over. A curious, terete foliaged plant, hanging in loose, straggling clumps. Flowers, white, lipwhite and purple—slightly fragrant.

A. virens

A very fine plant, native of Java. In growth and appearance very similar to A. *odoratum*. Raceme, many-flowered, drooping, produced in spring. Flowers medium-sized, very fragrant and long-lasting, white, flushed with rosy-purple; lip, large, spotted with crimson.

ANCISTROCHILUS

A small family of terrestrial orchids, natives of West Africa, which are allied to, and sometimes known as *Ipsea*. They require

ANGRAECUM HUMBLOTI (LEONIS)
Madagascar. Very much reduced.

planting in well-drained pots in an ordinary compost with the addition of some good loam, and are best accommodated in a warm position. During the growing season they require liberal waterings, but when this is complete they should be rested in a cool and light position.

A. Thomsoniana

Native of Tropical West Africa. A slender-growing plant, some eight inches high. Flower-spikes erect, produced in autumn, about one foot high, bearing several large white flowers in which the lip is blotched with rich purple. This plant is also known as *Ipsea Thomsoniana.*

ANGRÆCUM

A large family, chiefly natives of Madagascar, requiring warm treatment with plenty of water all the year round. They are epiphytes and may be cultivated in baskets or pots in broken crocks and moss. Never allow the plants to suffer from lack of water. Less is, of course, needed in dull, wet weather.

A. caudatum

Native of the West Coast of Africa. Stems erect, bearing two rows of recurved, dark green, strap-like leaves. The spikes are produced laterally in late summer and bear about five flowers. The latter are fairly large and slightly fragrant, dull brown. Lip, large, acute-pointed, pure white. Spur about eight inches long, brown.

A. eburnea

Native of Madagascar. Stems erect, stiff, some two feet or more high, bearing thick and leathery leaves. Flower spikes erect and many-flowered, borne in spring. The flowers are large and very fragrant, the narrow sepals and petals being of a curious greenish tint. Lip, pure white, large, cordate.

A. Leonis (*A. Humblotii*)

Madagascar. A very fine compact plant. Leaves fleshy thick, scimitar-like. Flower spike eight to ten inches long, bearing large white flowers. Lip, heart-shaped. Very handsome, and makes a good basket specimen.

A. sesquipedale

This is by far the largest and most showy of the family, and makes a handsome plant. Leaves, thick and leathery, one foot long, recurved. Flower spike, semi-erect, produced from the axils of the leaves in winter, three, to four, flowered. They are very large, often five or six inches across, pure white, fragrant and long-lasting. The spur to the labellum is very much elongated. Others include, *A. Ellisii*, *A. falcatum*, etc.

ANGULOA

A small family of showy-flowered epiphytal South American orchids. Flowers usually large and fragrant. They are best grown in pots in a mixture of moss, crocks, small pieces of charcoal, and some good loam. The roots should not be often disturbed so the pots may be of a fair size.

During the growing season they require plenty of water at the root, and when resting they should never be allowed to suffer from lack of water. They are not suited to warm localities.

A. Clowesii

This is about the best in the family. Native of Colombia. Pseudo-bulbs, fleshy; leaves, dark green, glossy and ribbed. Flowers large and fragrant, tulip-like, bright yellow. The column is white flushed with orange.

Others are :—*A. eburnea*, *A. Ruckeri*, etc., (the latter being a very showy orchid).

ANÆCTOCHILUS

A small family of terrestrial orchids, which are grown for their prettily-marked leaves. They are natives of tropical Asia, and one of the best species is found in Ceylon, 2,500 feet. They require to be grown in leaf-mould under shade with plenty of moisture at all seasons. Good drainage is essential.

A. regalis (wana rajah)

Native of Ceylon. Leaves velvety brown, thickly netted and meshed with gold. Flowers inconspicuous. Others include, *A. concinnus, A. Roxburghii.*

ARACHNANTHE

A fairly small family of tropical Asiatic epiphytal orchids, whose stems are usually tall and climbing. They may be grown up trees, or are very effective on arches and trellises. Leaves glossy, oblong-ovate. Thick white roots are produced freely from all up and down the stem. Flowers usually large and showy. They enjoy plenty of warmth and moisture during the growing period, with all available light.

A. Cathcartii

A large-growing, handsome plant from North India; enjoys plenty of warmth and moisture. Raceme axillary, strong and arching, bearing three to five large yellow flowers which are barred and mottled with brown.

A. Clarkei

Very similar in growth and habit to the foregoing, though the flowers are slightly smaller, but are more abundantly produced. India.

A. Lowii

A rather rare plant from Borneo, of stately habit. Stem erect, bearing two rows of long, drooping dark-green leaves. Flower spikes very long and drooping, five to eight feet, carrying a quantity of large yellowish-green flowers which are blotched with brownish-red. A quaint feature of this plant is that the two flowers first produced are larger than the rest and are brownish-yellow blotched with crimson. This species is of very slow growth and is not easy to manage.

A. moschifera

A rather scarce Javanese orchid, similar in growth to *A. Cathcartii.* Flowers pale yellow spotted with mauve, having a mush-like scent.

ARUNDINA

A pretty genus of reed-like terrestrial orchids, natives of the tropical parts of Asia.

A. bambusifolia

Stems two to three feet high with bamboo-like foliage. Flowers large, produced all the year round from the tops of the young growths, they are very like *Cattleyas* in shape and coloration, magenta rose, striped with orange in the throat. This plant may be grown in pots or in the open, it requires good loam, and enjoys liberal treatment when in full growth. A little liquid manure may be given with advantage when the buds are appearing. The flowers are not long-lasting, but this is made up for in the fact that several are borne in succession.

A. minor

Ceylon. Taller and reedier than the last. Flowers smaller and paler.

BLETIA

A fairly large genus of terrestrial, cool-climate orchids. They are of easy culture at the higher elevations, and enjoy good soil with plenty of water at the root when growing. After the flowering season is over and the leaves fall, they should be rested in a cool and airy position until the new growths appear in spring.

A. hyacinthina

Native of China. Very similar in growth to *Arundina bambusifolia,* but dwarfer. The flowers are borne on an upright basal spike and very like *Phaius* in shape. They are of medium size, and of a rosy mauve colour. Leaves ten inches or more long, deep nerved.

BRASSAVOLA

A curious family of epiphytal orchids from Tropical South America, related to the *Epidendrums, Cattleyas* and *Lælias.*

They are very amorphic and have, at times, been included among the *Lælias* and at others among the *Epidendrums.*

As a genus they are of very little merit—their culture is comparatively simple—but they have one great claim to notoriety in that one of them, *B. Digbyana* is usually used in obtaining the wonderful hybrids, *Brasso-Cattleya, Brasso-Catt-Lælia,* solely because of its very large spreading and fimbriated lip. This plant is usually the only one of the family that is ever cultivated.

B. Digbyana

A *Cattleya*-like orchid from British Honduras, which thrives under ordinary *Cattleya* treatment. Pseudo-bulbs, five inches high each, bearing one thick, leathery leaf. Leaf and pseudo-bulb are of a curious dull-purple.

Scape produced in autumn from the apex of the newly-ripened bulb—sheathed as in most of the *Cattleyas,* one-flowered. Flower, large, *Cattleya*-like, dull, greenish-white; lip, very large and spreading, pure-white, merging to green in the throat; very much fimbriated.

Lasts two or more weeks in bloom. Others are *B. ncdosa, B. lineata, B. venosa,* etc.

BRASSIA

A fairly large genus of epiphytal South American orchids which are not largely cultivated. They are easily grown at medium elevations in an ordinary compost if given plenty of water during the growing season. During the resting season they need less water, but should not be severely dried. The flowers of all this species are 'spidery' and of very quaint appearance.

B. maculata

Pseudo-bulbs oval and flattened, bearing two basal, lateral leaves and one apical leaf. They are deep green and leathery, recurved. Flowers, large and showy, yellow, blotched with brown; lip, white, spotted with purple.

B. verrucosa

Native of South America. Pseudo-bulbs pale green, fleshy. Leaves large, dark green, broad, acute-pointed. Flower scape long and many-flowered, borne in summer. The blooms are fairly large, sepals and petals pale green, blotched with deep purple. Lip white, bearing a quantity of green warts.

Others are :—*B. Lanceana, B. Caudata*, etc.

BULBOPHYLLUM

An extensive, though little grown genus of epiphytal old world orchids. They are confined to the warmer parts of Asia. They are of small growth, and the pseudo-bulbs are crowded, oval, one-or two-leafed. Flowers are usually borne on a slender stalk from the base of the mature pseudo-bulbs. They require basket treatment in a little ordinary open compost, with plenty of moisture and warmth. They do not require to be severely rested.

B. Dearei

Native of Borneo and the Philippine Islands. Pseudo-bulbs one inch in diameter, crowded, one-leafed. Flowers, two to three inches in length, borne on an arching wiry stem, orange-yellow with a darker meshing and netting of veins, blotched with purple.

B. elegans

A native of Ceylon, mid-country. Pseudo-bulbs small and wrinkled, Scape, one-leaved, one-flowered, produced in summer. Flowers, mauve, paler in the throat, where it is also striped with orange. A rather scarce species, quaint and very pretty.

B. Lobbii

A native of Burma, Java, etc., very similar to *B. Dearei*, but white, and the bulbs are spaced farther apart on the rhizome.

CALANTHE

The name (Beautiful Flower) is fully justified in this genus of terrestrial orchids, which are natives of tropical Asia and Australia.

The genus falls naturally into two distinct sections—deciduous and evergreen.

The deciduous section is of far more horticultural value and produces large, succulent pseudo-bulbs, bearing four, or more sword-like plaited leaves.

As the latter fall the flower-spikes appear. This section requires careful treatment, a good open compost, plenty of light and moisture while growing, with a distinct season of rest when the flowers have faded. At this time they should be placed (in their pots) in a cool light and airy position and again potted up when signs of new growth appear. The evergreen section throw up small pseudo-bulbs from a creeping rhizome and should be given a more loamy soil and plenty of pot room. They prefer a little more shading and do not require to be so severely rested. The evergreen section may be given weak doses of liquid manure weekly when the flower spikes appear.

C. purpurea

Native of Ceylon (4,000 feet), and India. Very handsome when in blossom. Flowers numerous, half an inch in diameter, purplish-pink; lip, lilac. They last long in flower. Leaves stalked two to three feet high, broad and acute-pointed.

C. veratrifolia

Also a native of Ceylon, growth and habit similar to the above. Flowers, pure white and exceptionally long-lasting, produced in quantities in June. Evergreen.

C. Vestita

Native of Burma. Flowers, large, pure white with a yellow stain on the lip. Deciduous. There are numerous varieties of this species—all beautiful, as are the many hybrids that have been raised.

CALANTHE PURPUREA

To face page 34

CATASETUM

A large genus of tropical South American epiphytal orchids. They require to be grown in well-drained pots or baskets in an open compost, and need liberal waterings in the growing season, and plenty of light, with a decided rest when this is complete. Pseudo-bulbs from four inches to two feet long, stem-like. Water must never be allowed to lodge in the young growths.

C. Bungerothii

Pseudo-bulbs, six inches high, tapering as they near the top. Leaves, few, ribbed, greyish-green; scape, semi-erect, bearing a few fairly large white flowers.

Sepals and petals lanceolate, acute-pointed. The dorsal sepal is hood-like. Lip, large, spathulate, has a crisped margin. A peculiar feature in these plants is their habit of ejecting the pollen masses if either of the two horn-like projections on the column is touched or irritated.

Others are :—*C. macrocarpum*, *C. longifolium*, etc.

CATTLEYA

A very extensive genus of large and showy-flowered South American orchids, all of which are epiphytes. The magnificently coloured and often very fragrant flowers are very large—in some kinds they exceed eight inches in diameter—and they are very long lasting.

With one or two exceptions they have stout creeping rhizomes from which the roots and swollen pseudo-bulbs are produced. The latter are usually produced annually from the growing point.

When once understood they are not hard to manage and thrive in pots or baskets which must be well drained. They enjoy a compost of chopped moss, decayed leaves and shredded bracken roots, to which must be liberally added finely broken crocks and charcoal, to keep it open and sweet.

When potting, the rhizome should rest on a little mound of compost slightly raised above the rim of the pot, and as they are vigorous growers the pots should be large enough to allow of about two years growth to form. During the growing season—when the new pseudo-bulbs are forming—they require plenty of light and air, with copious waterings at the root, particular care being taken that no water is allowed to remain in the young pseudo-bulbs or in their protecting sheaths, or again, in the sheaths that envelope the flower scapes, as they are very liable to damp off and die—I have lost several growths in this manner. When growth is complete they should be kept in a dry, cool, and airy position to mature the pseudo-bulbs—and thus ensure their flowering (but they must not be over-dried). When the flower-spikes appear, they must again be given liberal treatment and encouraged in every way to produce strong spikes.

They are exceptionally beautiful plants, and are well worth the little extra care that can be given them. As there are several hundreds of species and hybrids, space will not permit of more than a few of the best known species being described.

C. citrina

A very unusual type of *Cattleya*, producing globular pseudo-bulbs. The plant is suited to high elevations and should be grown on a block well covered with moss and kept damp. Flowers, yellow, drooping, scented. The plant should be suspended upside down.

C. labiata

Native of Brazil, bearing large one-leaved pseudo-bulbs some six inches high, from the apices of which the flower-spikes of large rosy crimson and yellow blossoms are produced in autumn. The large folded labellum is of a deep, velvety crimson, bordered with white, and has a blotch of yellow in the throat. They are some five to six inches in diameter.

C. Mendellii

A magnificent plant with short, sturdy pseudo-bulbs, native of Colombia. The flowers, which are borne in early summer, are large, pure white, delicately flushed with rose, and of a satiny sheen. The spreading lip is crimson-purple, blotched in the throat with deep yellow. The flowers frequently exceed seven inches in diameter.

C. Mossiæ

A very fine Brazilian species which produces its large lilac and rosy-purple flowers in spring. The pseudo-bulbs are strong and

Photo kindly lent by Messrs. J. A. MacBean, England

A HYBRID CATTLEYA

To face page 36

furrowed and bear one thick, leathery leaf. The beautifully-fringed large labellum is veined and flushed with deep purple and has an orange blotch at the base.

C. Warscewiczii (*C. gigas, &c.*)

One of the best in the family. The flowers are borne on an erect spike in summer and are often eight inches or more in diameter. The sepals and petals are pale purplish-rose, while the large and spreading labellum is crimson-purple with a large blotch of deep yellow in the throat. Pseudo-bulbs, eight inches long, furrowed, and one-leaved. A really magnificent orchid.

There are numerous species and hybrids, and with a little care a selection of these may be had in flower for the greater part of the year, while all of them are beautiful. They are best grown where the temperature varies between sixty-five degrees and eighty degrees. The hybrids of this genus are very fine indeed, and are for the most part, very easy to manage. *All* are well worth cultivating.

CHYSIS

A small family of showy-flowered, epiphytal orchids from South America. They are best accommodated in baskets in an ordinary compost, and enjoy warmth and plenty of water when in full growth; after this is complete they should be given a cooler and drier position, but do not need severe resting. They are impatient of water lodging in the young growths.

C. bractescens

This is perhaps the finest of the genus. Pseudo-bulbs four to ten inches high, fleshy, spindle-shaped, bearing broad, elongated leaves. Flower racemes produced in spring with the new growths; they bear three or more "cupped" yellow flowers, the sepals and petals being tipped with crimson. They are some four inches across, and are backed by long bracts.

CIRRHOPETALUM

A fairly large genus of tropical old world orchids, very similar in growth, habit, and requiring the same treatment as advised for *Bulbophyllum*. They are all epiphytes.

C. grandiflorum

A native of Ceylon (4,500 feet). Rather scarce. Pseudo-bulbs one inch high, one-leafed, borne on a creeping rhizome at intervals of about three inches. Leaves apical, solitary, about four inches long, dark green and leathery. The flowers are produced in summer from the bases of the mature pseudo-bulbs on slender stalks about five inches long, two-flowered. The latter are tawny yellow, the twisted petals being about two and a half inches in length, blotched and striped with crimson and purple. The lip is deep purple—so finely balanced that the least movement will set it rocking.

C. Macræi

Another Ceylon orchid (2,000 feet), very similar in growth, etc., to the above, except that the flowers are smaller and paler, while the lip is pale yellow.

CŒLOGYNE

An extensive genus of large-flowered and showy orchids. They are all epiphytes and are natives of Asia, Malaysia, etc.

It is a most useful genus—surely everyone knows the lovely *C. cristata* which is in so constant a demand at home for bouquets, decorations, etc., while there are several other exceedingly pretty and useful species to be found in the family.

They may be grown in well-drained pots or baskets in the ordinary compost advised for epiphytes, and require plenty of water during the growing season—care being taken that water is not allowed to stand in the young shoots as they are very liable to damp off. Shading from bright sun is very beneficial.

Those that produce their flowers on long, drooping racemes are best accommodated in hanging baskets which will thus show off the flowers to perfection.

C. asperata

A very fine, large-growing, tropical species from Borneo. Pseudo-bulbs four inches high, oblong and furrowed, bearing two apical, stalked leaves, which are one foot or more in length, broad and ribbed. The flower raceme is produced from the apex of the new pseudo-bulb with the leaves and is many-flowered, semi-erect.

They are very fragrant, some two inches or more in diameter, pure white, the lip being blotched with brown and streaked with yellow, while the margin is beautifully crisped.

C. cristata

A well-known and showy-flowered species from India. Pseudo-bulbs smooth, elongated, glossy, two-leaved. The raceme is drooping and many-flowered, bearing large, pure white flowers some three inches in diameter. The large frilled lip has a blotch of golden yellow. This species does not require much heat, and will not thrive in the low-country.

C. Dayana

A very handsome orchid from Borneo, requiring a hot, steamy atmosphere with plenty of water during active growth. It may be grown in pots or hanging baskets as the racemes are long and pendent. Pseudo-bulbs pear-shaped, five inches high, bearing two stalked, pointed, oval, ribbed leaves. The many-flowered raceme is borne in summer and is often three feet long. The flowers are some two inches across, pale yellow. The trilobed lip is large, streaked and zoned with rich brown.

C. elata

Northern India. A cool-climate orchid. Pseudo-bulbs oblong, four inches high, furrowed and two-leafed, the flower spike is erect, and is produced with the leaves in spring. The flowers are medium-sized, white, with a yellow band on the lip.

C. flaccida

Native of India. Pseudo-bulbs three inches high, pointed, two-leafed. The flowers are borne in winter on a drooping, many-flowered raceme. They are fairly large, white, lip stained with yellow. The withered appearance of the scales at the bases of the racemes gives rise to the specific name.

C. fuscescens

A very fine species from India and Burma. Pseudo-bulbs, six inches long, cylindrical and of a semi-climbing habit, bearing two oval, ribbed leaves some six inches long. The raceme of large reddish-yellow flowers is produced in winter from the apex of the ripened pseudo-bulb. The lip is streaked with yellow and has two blotches of brown on the front lobe.

C. longipes

Native of Northern India and Darjeeling. Pseudo-bulbs are borne on a creeping rhizome at intervals of about two inches. They are smooth, three inches high and compressed. The two apical leaves are four to six inches long, strap-shaped and acute-pointed. The erect scape is borne in late summer with the leaves from the apices of the new pseudo-bulbs, two-flowered. The flowers are some two and a half inches in diameter, and of a pale ochre yellow. Sepals blunt, ovate, larger than the petals, which are acute-pointed. Lip large, tri-lobed: side lobes nearly white curving towards the column. The spreading front lobe is beautifully veined and meshed with rich brown, and has two ridges, or crests of the same colour running its entire length. The margin is delicately fringed with fine brown hairs. Column, lemon-yellow, club-shaped; has a blotch of brown at the base. Owing to the climbing habit of this plant it should be grown in long baskets that allow plenty of room for the rhizome and pseudo-bulbs to develop—in a compost of chopped moss and finely broken crocks. It requires moisture at all seasons, and should be kept in a shady position. It may also be grown with great success if the creeping rhizomes are twined round a portion of a branch, say two feet high, placed upright in a pot.

In this case however, moss should be tied on to the branch to form a rooting medium.

C. Massangeana

A fine species (very similar to *C. asperata*) from Assam. Racemes, many-flowered, long and pendulous. Flowers, large, pale-yellow; lip, rich brown, streaked, and blotched with yellow.

C. ocellata

A small-growing, pretty little species from Northern India. It is well adapted to basket culture and does not require much heat. Pseudo-bulbs spheroid, glossy, two-leafed. The flower spike is produced with the new foliage from the apices of the young pseudo-bulbs in spring. The flowers are fairly large and fragrant, pure white; the lip has two blotches of yellow on the front lobe (hence the specific name).

C. odoratissima

Native of the up-country jungles of Ceylon (4,500 feet), and Southern India. It is a small-growing, compact orchid. Pseudo-bulbs crowded and wrinkled, barely one inch in diameter, each bearing two narrow, grassy leaves, two inches long. The three-flowered raceme is borne apically in spring from the new pseudo-bulbs. The flowers are large for the size of the plant, pure white and fragrant; lip, stained with lemon-yellow or orange. Well adapted for culture in baskets, and very free-flowering. This species requires a fairly cool climate with plenty of water at all seasons.

C. pandurata

An exceptionally fine species from Java, Malaya, etc., that requires a hot, moist climate with shade all the year round. Pseudo-bulbs four to six inches long by three inches in diameter, curiously flattened and slightly furrowed; they occur at intervals of about three inches on the stout creeping rhizome. They bear two long-ribbed leaves and the erect, many-flowered raceme is borne apically in early summer. The flowers are large, some three inches or more in diameter, and of a bright green colour, very fragrant. The long lip has several velvety-black ridges running its entire length. The flowers are very long-lasting and showy and the plant is one that merits every attention. It is best grown in baskets that allow plenty of room for the rhizome and pseudo-bulbs to develop, any ordinary, well-drained compost suiting it.

C. Parishii

A pretty little species that much resembles *C. fuscescens* in growth and appearance, but is smaller, while the flowers are very like those of *C. pandurata*, but again smaller. They are borne on an erect raceme in summer. Native of Burma.

Other species which are well worth growing include *C. decipiens*, *C. flavida*, *C. lentiginosa*, *C. ochracea*, etc.

COTTONIA

A small family of Vanda-like orchids. The one mentioned here is about the only one in cultivation. It is an epiphyte and requires the same treatment as *Aerides.*

C. macrostachya

Native of Ceylon (low-country) and India. Leaves thick and channelled. Flowers fairly small, on an erect raceme ; dull orange, veined with red ; somewhat resembling an insect.

CRYPTOCHILUS

A small family of terrestrial tropical Asiatic orchids. Easily grown at medium and high elevations, in pots of good loamy soil, under light shade. Plenty of moisture is necessary.

C. Arachnites

A native of Ceylon (4,000 feet), non-pseudo-bulbous. Leaves stalked, six inches high, heart-shaped and acute-pointed, pale green on the upper surface, shaded with deep purple on the under side. Spike erect, many-flowered, one foot high, produced in spring and summer. The flowers are medium-sized, of spiky appearance, greenish-purple. The large lip is lilac, spotted with purple.

CYCNOCHES

A fairly small species of tropical epiphytal South American orchids. They are of easy culture and may be grown in pots or baskets (well-drained) of bracken roots and moss, with the addition of some clean sand. During the growing season they should be liberally watered, and, as they are deciduous they should be given a long period of rest when the leaves have dropped, but should again be watered freely when the new growth is observed.

C. chlorochilon

A very graceful, showy, and large-flowered species. Pseudo-bulbs fleshy, ten inches high, clothed with the old leaf sheathes. Leaves apical, ribbed, and strap-like ; ten inches long. The flowers which are borne on an arching scape are about five inches in diameter and of a pale greeny-yellow. Lip, large, pure white; has a blotch of metallic green in the centre.

Others include:—*C. aureum*, *C. Ventricosum*, etc.

CYMBIDIUM

A useful, large, and easily grown family of terrestrial and epiphytal orchids, natives of India, Burma, Ceylon, Java, Malaya, etc. They may be grown in pots or baskets in the same compost as recommended for *Cœlogynes*, with the addition of some good fibrous loam and rotton cow manure. The foliage is usually erect and sword-like, while the flowers are generally large, showily coloured and long-lasting. Non-pseudo-bulbous, they require plenty of water at the root all the year round and do not need to be rested in any way, save that a reduced supply of water will be necessary during the resting season. Shading from the hot sun is beneficial, and great heat is not essential.

C. bicolor

Native of Ceylon (low and mid-country). Leaves, stiff and narrow; racemes, pendent, many-flowered, borne at different seasons of the year. The latter are one and a half inches in diameter, creamy-yellow, veined with dull purple, resembling an insect.

C. Cyperifolium

A native of Northern India, which I believe to be identical with *C. ensifolium* (which see).

C. Devonianum

A pretty species from Northern India. Leaves stalked, spathulate, eight inches high. Racemes arching and many-flowered; produced in early spring. The flowers are medium-sized, pale yellowish-brown, streaked and blotched with purple; lip, white, veined with purple, the throat being of the latter colour.

C. eburneum

A large-growing and very beautiful species from Northern India. Leaves ensiform, narrow, slightly drooping, borne from a sort of pseudo-bulb. Flower-spike erect, few-flowered, produced in winter and spring. The flowers are large and very fragrant, some two and a half inches in diameter, pure white. The lip is suffused with pale yellow, and there are a few very faint blotches of pale purple on the bases of the sepals and petals. This species is well adapted to culture at medium and high elevations.

C elegans

(See *Cyperorchis elegans*).

C. ensifolinm

A pretty little free-flowering orchid, native of Ceylon (3,500 feet) and Sikkim. Leaves narrow, fairly stiff, grassy. Scape semi-erect, two feet or more high, many-flowered. The latter are produced in spring and summer. They are one and a half inches across, very fragrant, pale yellow striped with red, and some orange on the lip.

C. giganteum

A large-growing handsome species from Northern India. Leaves, two feet long by two inches wide, drooping; produced in a distichous manner from a sort of pseudo-bulb. Flower-spike strong and arching, many-flowered, produced in winter. The large brown flowers, often four inches across, are streaked with red, while the yellow lip is blotched and spotted with crimson. This species makes a handsome specimen if well treated.

C. Lowianum

An extraordinarily fine plant from Burma and a great favourite when in flower in the spring. The narrow, grassy leaves are ensiform, two feet high. Flower-spike is semi-erect and many-flowered—often literally clothed with large, yellowish-green flowers which are streaked with brown (they are often four inches across). The large yellow lip bears a blotch of purple-brown on the front lobe.

This species requires practically unlimited water during the growing season, and a little liquid manure given when the flower spikes are forming will be very beneficial. It prefers a temperature of seventy degrees or less.

C. Parishii

A beautiful but rather scarce species from Burma. Leaves thick and rigid, one to two feet high, dark green, ensiform. The

CYPREPEDIUM HIRSUTISSIMUM **(Natural Size)** *See page* 49

To face page 45

erect, few-flowered spike is borne in autumn. The flowers are large and fragrant, creamy white, the lip being banded with yellow and spotted with purple.

C. Tracyanum

This is about the largest-flowered species in the genus, for they often measure over five inches across. In habit and growth it is very similar to *C. grandiflorum*, while the flowers are much like those of *C. ensifolium*, but, of course, very much larger. Sepals and petals pale yellow, striped longitudinally with red ; lip large, trilobed, side lobes, yellow, striped with red. Middle lobe very pale yellow, spotted with red. Column, greenish-yellow.

Other fine species include :—*C. aloifolium, C. insigne, C. Munronianum, C. Simonsianum, C. Finlaysonianum*, etc., the latter being a very large and showy orchid.

CYPERORCHIS

A small family of terrestrial orchids, natives of Asia, nearly allied to *Cymbidiums* and requiring the same treatment.

C. elegans (*cymbidium elegons*)

Native of India. Leaves narrow, stiff, eighteen inches high. The semi-erect scape is many-flowered and is produced in winter. The flowers are medium-sized, creamy-white, and never fully open. The other species is :—*C. Mastersii*, India, flowers, pale-pink, etc.

CYPREPEDIUM

This is the correct name for the Lady's Slipper Orchid and the family is a very large one, confined to tropical Asia ; its allies, the *Selenepediums* being natives of the new world. The culture of both families is the same, but as they are slightly different in the structure of the flowers, etc., I have not included the *Selenepediums* under this heading. They may be either terrestrial or epiphytic are non-pseudo-bulbous and well adapted to pot culture. The pots should be clean and well-drained with a sufficiency of broken crocks and lime rubble, and the compost that seems to suit them well is made from a mixture of moss, shredded, bracken roots and fibrous loam, which must be kept open and porous by the addition of some clean sharp sand and finely broken charcoal.

They require fair shading with plenty of moisture during the growing season, and, although they need less water after the flowering period, they should never be dried in any way. The leaves are usually long and strap-shaped, while the erect scapes are produced from the centres of the newly developed off-shoots and are often three or more flowered. The latter are often very large and the sepals are sometimes long and twisted. The lip is almost invariably large and pouched, highly coloured, while they are very long-lasting in full beauty. In a word, they are easily managed and very showy orchids that seem to flower regularly with very little attention. Water must not be allowed to lodge in the young growth, and for this reason it is better to use a watering-can in preference to the syringe.

Their name is legion, for there are several hundreds of species and hybrids, so I shall have to confine my descriptions to a few of the better known and more showy species.

C. barbatum

Native of Malaya. Leaves eight inches long, prettily blotched with dark green on a lighter ground. Scape, erect, one-flowered, produced in winter. The flowers are large; dorsal sepal white, green and purple, other sepals and petals similarly coloured, and bear dark shining warts from which tufts of black hairs are borne. Lip large, helmet-like, purplish-black.

C. bellatulum

A very pretty species from Upper Burma. Leaves beautifully marked with olive and dark green; purple on the under side: eight to ten inches long, thick and leathery. Scapes erect, four inches high, one-flowered; produced at different seasons of the year. Flowers three to four inches across, pure white, thickly spotted and blotched with purplish-black. Lip, small. This species likes a little more light than the rest, and the addition of some lime rubble to the compost is supposed to be beneficial.

C. Boxalli

Another beautiful Burmese species. Leaves one foot long, bright green, narrow, strap-like. Scape erect, bearing one or two large flowers in spring. They are greenish-yellow tinged with purple; the whole flower has a glazed appearance. Best suited to high and medium elevations.

C. callosum

A handsome species from Assam. Leaves, stiff, mottled with two shades of green; eight inches long. Flowers, medium-sized, very showy; white, shaded with deep purple and green. Lip, medium-sized, brownish-purple and green. They are borne in summer.

C. concolor

A pretty little species from the same habitat as the preceding. Leaves, dark green mottled with grey. Scape, one-flowered, short, and erect, produced in winter. Flowers, creamy-yellow, spotted with reddish-brown. Lip, small.

C. Curtisii

A fine species from Java and Sumatra. Leaves, pale green, mottled with olive. Flowers, large, borne on an erect stem, ten inches high in summer. They are green and mauve, sepals slightly hairy. Pouch, large, deep purple, netted, and veined with black.

C. Fairieanum

An exceedingly showy-flowered but slow-growing species that came originally (I believe) from Assam. It was, at one time, one of the most expensive and rare orchids; and I believe I am right in saying that over £1,000 has been offered for a plant in the past. It requires to be grown in a light, open and well-drained compost or fine bracken roots, broken charcoal and some fibrous loam. Shading in bright weather is very necessary. Leaves, eight inches long, deep-green, acute-pointed. Scape, eight to ten inches high, one-flowered; borne in winter. The flowers are fairly large; the dorsal sepal is white, shaded with green, and streaked with purple. The petals are of the same colour, hairy, turned up at the ends. Pouch, large, purple, shaded with brown, and netted with green. I have before me a list of orchids from an Eastern Firm and this orchid is quoted among them, so it would seem that its habitat has been re-discovered.

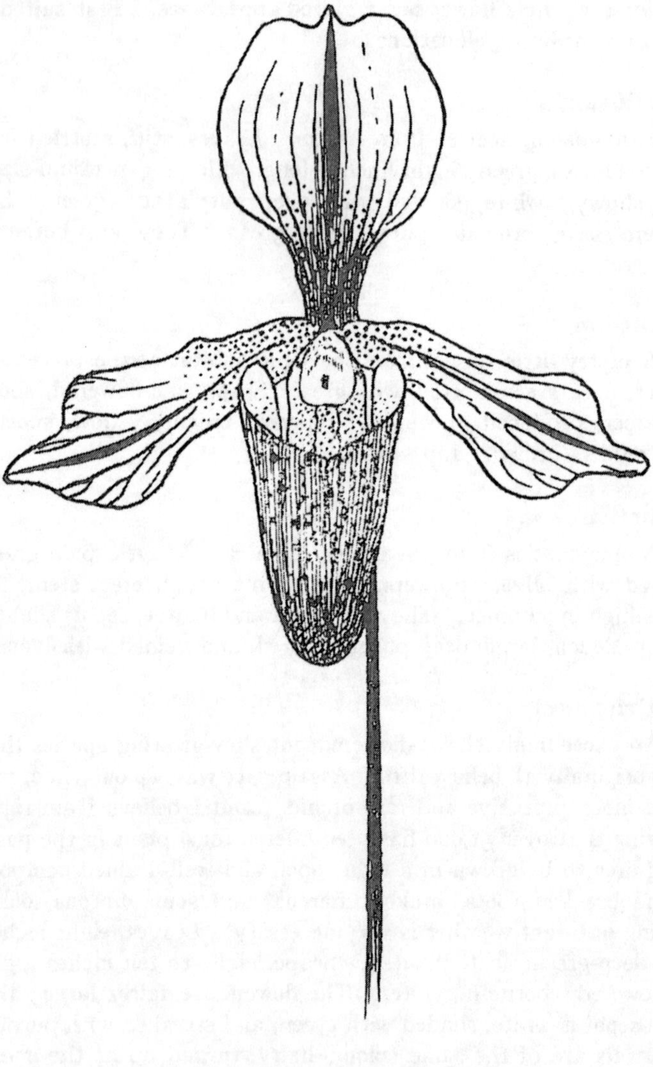

CYPREPEDIUM SPICERIANUM

C. hirsutissimum

A large-growing species from Northern India and Upper Burma. Leaves in a compact tuft, one foot or more long, strap-shaped and acute-pointed, pale green. Flower-scape erect, one foot high, hairy ; bearing in spring a single large flower, often six inches or more across. They are deep purple and green with pale green margins to the sepals. The large pouch is deep green with purple shading. An exceptionally fine plant.

C. insigne

A well-known plant and one that seems to be commonly cultivated. It is easy to grow and flowers regularly in winter. Leaves pointed, eight inches long, pale green. Scapes, single-flowered, erect, one foot high. Flowers three inches or more across, bright green and glossy, irregularly blotched and veined with purple. Pouch greenish brown. This species does not require great heat.

C. Lawrenceanum

A fine Bornean species with handsome, variegated foliage. Scapes, sturdy, erect, bearing one large flower in early summer. The flowers are brightly coloured, white, green and yellow, the pouch being very large. This plant likes plenty of warmth.

C. Parishii

A handsome, strong-growing species from Burma, which produces its large flowers on an erect, branching scape in autumn. Leaves, thick and leathery, deep-green, three inches wide and ten inches long. Scape, stout and hairy, four-to five-flowered, two feet or more in height. Flowers, two and a half inches across, with a long purple and green pouch. Sepals, pale yellow, with green and mauve veins. The great feature in this species is the length of the petals, which are often over seven inches long, curiously twisted. They are pale green, warted, and hairy, deep purple at the apices.

C. Spicerianum

A beautiful little orchid, native of Burma. Leaves, six inches long, pale green, acute-pointed, dotted with purple on the under side. Scape, erect, one-flowered, six inches high; produced in summer. Flowers, two to three inches in diameter, purple, green and violet. Pouch, large, dull purplish-brown.

C. Stonei

A very handsome species from British North Borneo. Leaves, dull green, leathery, one foot long. Scape often eighteen inches to two feet high, branching; bearing two or three flowers in early winter. They are large and showy, pure white, shaded with yellow and veined with purple.

The sepals are nearly five inches long, narrow and twisted. Pouch large, dull brownish-red veined with purple.

C. superbiens.

Native of Java. Leaves dull green, beautifully shaded and mottled with deep green, presenting a marbled appearance. Scape erect, one-flowered, ten inches high, produced in summer.

The flowers are large, white, green and purple, finely-veined with deep purple and green. Pouch large and open, dull brown-purple.

C. venustum.

A dwarf-growing handsome little plant from Assam. Leaves, short and thick, mottled like those of *C. bellatulum*; purple underneath. The short scapes bear a single medium-sized flower early in the year. The latter are greenish-white, flushed with pink and veined with green. The petals are veined with, and bear numerous purple warts. Pouch, green, veined with deeper green and shaded with purple.

C. villosum.

A beautiful and easily-grown plant, native of Burma. Leaves, leathery; bright green, one foot or more long. Flowers on tall, erect, and hairy scapes in spring. They are large, brown-purple and green. The dorsal sepal is hairy; purple-green and white. The whole flower appears to have been varnished, and is very striking.

There are some very fine hybrid *Cypripediums*, and among them may be particularly mentioned the following showy-flowered varieties :—

C. Adrastus: C. Boxalli × *C. Leeanum*
C. Ashburtoniæ: C. barbatum × *C. insigne*
C. Gaskelliana: C. Spicerianum × *C. Fairieanum*

C. Harrisianum: C. villosum × C. barbatum
C. Minos: C. Spicerianum × C. Arthurianum
C. Superciliare: C. superbiens × C. barbatum
C. T. B. Haywood: C. Druryi × C. superbiens

The whole family may be increased by separating the growths, i.e., taking off a new growth on its own roots (during the growing season) and potting it up separately. They should be kept shaded and on the dry side until the roots take hold of the compost.

DENDROBIUM

A very large family of epiphytal orchids which are practically confined to the tropical parts of the old world, though a few have been found in tropical Australia. A selection of *Dendrobiums* would give a very fine collection of orchids and one that might be expected to produce flowers throughout the year. They are all sun-and warmth-loving plants and are naturally found growing on trees or in crevices of rocks where they obtain little or no shading. They are all pseudo-bulbous, but differ enormously in growth, size, etc., though the flowers are all formed on one plan. There must be several hundreds of known *Dendrobes,* and certainly well over a hundred are cultivated. In some, the pseudo-bulbs are tall and woody, in others short and fleshy. They are often bamboo-like and bear leaves either apical or lateral, while in some species, they are one-leafed. The leaves may be broad or grassy, deciduous or persistent.

The flowers are usually large, highly-coloured and fragrant, the labellum always ending in a sort of spur at the back. They are almost invariably produced in clusters of two or more from the apices or sides of the ripened pseudo-bulbs, or in apical spikes.

They may be cultivated in pots or baskets—the latter are best for the delicate kinds, while such strong growers as *D. thyrsiflorum, D. fimbriatum, D. densiflorum, D. calceolare,* etc., are best accommodated in pots.

They all require a light, open compost which must be well-drained, and very little of it is necessary. They enjoy liberal treatment in the growing season with plenty of light and warmth, but when growth is complete they should be given a long period of rest with drier and cooler conditions. As the flower buds appear they must again have every encouragement. The evergreen species—*D. thyrsiflorum, D. densiflorum, D. Phalænopsis,* etc. should not be rested so severely as the others, and they need a little more shading.

D. aureum

A pretty little Ceylon and Indian species, at elevations of about 4,000 feet. Pseudo-bulbs, long and drooping, sometimes erect, "jointed," yellowish when old. Leaves, lanceolate, deciduous, grassy. The flowers are borne in twos and threes from the "joints" of the mature pseudo-bulbs in spring and summer. They are pale yellow, primrose-scented. The large, drooping and tongued lip has a blotch of orange in the throat. This species is well adapted to culture in baskets.

Variety—*D. a. giganteum* (Burma) has larger flowers and an orange-stained lip with a blotch of red in the throat. It does not need such cool conditions as the type.

D. amœnum

A slender-growing species from Northern India. Pseudo-bulbs thin, two feet long, purplish-brown; leaves, grassy, deciduous. Flowers are borne in twos and threes from the "joints" of the mature pseudo-bulbs in spring; they are white, tipped with purple, with a delicious violet-like scent.

D. aggregatum

Northern India and Burma. Pseudo-bulbs oblong, one inch long, swollen and furrowed, one-leafed. Flowers are borne in an arching raceme some six inches long from the mature pseudo-bulbs in early summer. They are about two inches across; deep orange-yellow.

D. albo-songuineum

A very fine large-flowered species from Lower Burma. Pseudo-bulbs erect, eight inches long, thick; yellow when mature. Leaves, lanceolate, deciduous, before the flowers appear in spring. The latter are borne on axillary racemes of three or four, and are very large, often four inches or more in diameter, creamy-white and waxy textured. The sepals and petals are blotched with maroon, while the large spreading lip bears two blotches of crimson-brown. It lasts a long time in full flower.

D. cariniferum

An evergreen sturdy orchid from Burma. The erect pseudo-bulbs are six inches to ten inches high, hairy; leaves, lanceolate, two inches long, persistent for two years. Flowers are borne in tufts from the apices of the mature pseudo-bulbs. They are pure white with an orange-brown crest.

D. chrysanthum

A large-growing, deciduous species from India and Burma. Pseudo-bulbs thick and drooping, often five feet long. The flowers are fragrant, borne in clusters of three or more from the young leafy pseudo-bulbs in late summer. They are some one and a half inches in diameter, and of a deep golden yellow. The downy lip has two purple blotches in the throat. This species is best grown in hanging baskets.

D. calceolare

A large-growing, sturdy, evergreen orchid from India. Pseudo-bulbs bamboo-like, erect and woody, bearing two rows of oblong, lanceolate, persistent leaves. Flowers are borne in semi-erect terminal racemes in spring, of ten, or more. They are fairly large, creamy-yellow, and orange.

D. chrysotoxum

A fine species from Burma. Pseudo-bulbs eight inches to ten inches long, swollen in the centre, furrowed, bearing four to five apical, large, leathery leaves which are persistent for two years. The arching raceme, bearing several large golden-yellow flowers is produced in early summer from near the apices of the mature pseudo-bulbs. The large lip is fringed, and has a streak of blood-red in the throat. There are several distinct varieties of this species—all beautiful.

D. Cœlogyne

A very large-flowered species from Lower Burma. Pseudo-bulbs very thick and fleshy ; two inches long, bearing three or four apical broad leaves. Flowers pale yellow, blotched with red ; lip deep purple. The flower is very much like a *Cœlogyne* in shape.

D. crassinode (Syn: *D. pendulum*)

A very quaint species from Burma, free-flowering and deciduous. Pseudo-bulbs, semi-erect or pendent; nodes very much swollen. Leaves, lanceolate, three inches long, deciduous before the flowers appear in spring. The flowers are borne in groups of two or three from the nodes of the ripened pseudo-bulbs, and are white, flushed with rose and tipped with amethyst. Lip, yellow-margined with white, and tipped with purple; slightly fragrant.

D. crepidatum

A small, delicate species from Burma. Pseudo-bulbs semi-erect, one foot long, as thick as a pencil, pale green and fleshy, striped with white. Leaves two inches long, deciduous, narrow. Flowers medium-sized, produced in twos or threes from the nodes of the ripened pseudo-bulbs in early spring. They are white, tipped with pale rose.

D. crumenatum (White Dove Orchid.)

A pretty little orchid, native of Ceylon (low-country) and Java. Pseudo-bulbs one foot high, thin at the base, swollen in the centre, extending to a long, quill-like end. Leaves, small, ovate, thick and deciduous. The small, white and fragrant flowers are borne in quantity at different seasons of the year. They are supposed to resemble a dove, and seem to never fully open.

D. Crystallinum

A pretty and free-flowering species from Burma, that never fails to bear its quantities of delicately-tinted flowers in spring. Pseudo-bulbs one foot long, leaves lance-shaped, three inches long, deciduous. Flowers borne in twos and threes from the joints of the ripened leafless pseudo-bulbs in spring. They are about one and a half inches in diameter, white, flushed with rose and tipped with amethyst. Lip, pale yellow with a blotch of mauve in front.

D. Dearei

An exceptionally fine evergreen species from the Philippine Islands. Pseudo-bulbs erect and sturdy, one foot high, clothed with oval, dark-green, persistent leaves. The flowers are borne in apical bunches of five or more in summer and are some two inches in diameter, pure white and fragrant. The large, tongue-shaped lip is stained with green. They are extremely long-lasting, and the plants are admirably suited for indoor decoration. I have had two plants in full flower for over two months. This species requires very hot and moist conditions and prefers basket treatment.

D. Dalhousieanum (*D. Pulchellum.*)

A very handsome species from Northern India. Pseudo-bulbs strong, semi-erect, eighteen inches long, bearing blunt, oval, deciduous leaves four inches long. The flowers are very large, some five inches across, and are produced in clusters from near the apices of the ripened pseudo-bulbs. They are pale yellow flushed with pink : the large lip has two blotches of crimson in the throat. This species is very beautiful but seems rather shy-flowering.

D. densiflorum

A sturdy, evergreen orchid from Burma, very nearly allied to *D. thyrsiflorum.* Pseudo-bulbs, erect, eighteen inches high, narrow at the base, swollen and angled above, bearing about four broad, apical leaves. The flowers are produced in early summer from near the tops of the pseudo-bulbs on densely clothed drooping racemes of forty or fifty flowers which are fairly large and fragrant; deep yellow.

PORTION OF FLOWER-SPIKE. DENDROBIUM DEAREI (Nat. Size)

To face page 56

The lip is velvety and of a deeper colour than the rest of the flower. A large plant in full flower is a magnificent sight.

Variety—*Schroderianum.* Very similar to *D. thyrsiflorum.* Flowers loosely set, white and yellow.

D. Devonianum

An extremely pretty plant from Northern India. Pseudo-bulbs, long, drooping, and slender, some three feet or more in length. Leaves, grassy, deciduous, before the flowers appear in early summer. The latter are produced in great quantity from the nodes of the ripened pseudo-bulbs. They are some two inches in diameter, cream-coloured, tinted with pale rose and fragrant. The lip is large, with a fringed margin, white, and has a blotch of orange in the throat. The flowers last about two weeks, and when in flower this plant is very pretty.

D. dixanthum

A pretty little species, rather scarce, native of Burma. Pseudo-bulbs, quill-like, reddish-brown when mature. Leaves, grassy, deciduous. The flowers are produced in groups of two or three in autumn from the nodes of the ripened pseudo-bulbs, two inches or three inches in diameter, pale yellow throughout. They are fragrant and long-lasting.

D. draconis

A sturdy evergreen species, native of Burma. Pseudo-bulbs, one foot high, slightly hairy: leaves, three inches long, oblong, lanceolate. The flowers are borne in clusters from the top joints of the ripened pseudo-bulbs, and are about two inches across. They are pure white, the lip is crested, striped with orange-red. This species flowers freely and regularly every spring.

D. Falconeri

Another very pretty and graceful species from Upper Burma, that enjoys basket treatment and a fairly cool position. Pseudo-bulbs, slender, pendent, very much knotted and branched. Leaves thin and grassy, deciduous. Flowers are borne freely from the nodes of the mature pseudo-bulbs in early summer. They are

DENDROBIUM FORMOSUM GIGANTEUM.

fairly large, white, flushed with rosy purple. Lip, large, mauve, with two blotches of orange on the front lobe, margined with white and tipped with reddish-purple.

D. Farmeri

An evergreen, erect plant from India and Burma. Pseudo-bulbs, eight inches high, erect, thin at the base, much swollen and distinctly quadrangular above, bearing three or four blunt, oblong, deep-green leaves. The flowers are borne in a pendulous raceme in spring from the tops of the ripened pseudo-bulbs, much as in *D. densiflorum* (but more loosely set), pale yellow, flushed with pink, the lip being a deep velvety yellow.

D. Findlayanum

A quaint but very handsome species from Burma. Pseudo-bulbs one foot high, semi-erect. The internodes are narrow while the nodes are curiously flattened; they are bright yellow and bear pale green deciduous leaves. The flowers are produced in early summer, singly or in twos, from the nodes of the mature pseudo-bulbs. They are fair sized, lavender-coloured; the large lip is deep yellow bordered with white.

D. fimbriatum

A well-known, erect-growing species from India and Burma. Pseudo-bulbs three feet or more high; bamboo-like and woody, clothed with lanceolate leaves which are persistent for a considerable time. The flowers are produced in loose, pendulous racemes from the tops of the ripened pseudo-bulbs in spring. They are two and a half inches in diameter and deep orange. Lip beautifully fringed and velvety.

Variety.—*D. f. oculatum* has a blotch of deep purple in the throat.

D. formosum giganteum

An extremely showy-flowered white species from Burma. The stout, woody pseudo-bulbs are erect, one foot high, covered with black hairs and bearing two rows of blunt, shining leaves. The flowers are borne in clusters of three or more at different seasons (chiefly perhaps in summer and autumn) from the apices of the young, leafy pseudo-bulbs. They are very large and long-lasting, pure white, often five inches in diameter. The large and spreading lip is deeply cleft and has a blotch of yellow in the centre. This is a very fine orchid, and is not hard to grow. It does not need very severe resting.

D. lituiflorum

A slender-growing dendrobe from Northern India and Burma. Pseudo-bulbs, greyish, drooping, two feet long. Leaves deciduous. Flowers in pairs from the nodes of ripened pseudo-bulbs after a rest. Flowers two feet or more across, rosy-purple. Lip trumpet-shaped, (Lat. *lituus*). Purple and white.

D. Lyoni

Of very distinct character as to growth and flowers for a *dendrobe.* Native of the Philippine Islands.

Pseudo-bulbs two to three inches high, globose and distinctly four-angled, bearing two apical leaves some eight inches or more long; very similar to some of the *Cœlogynes.*

The drooping flower-spike is borne from the apices of the newly-ripened pseudo-bulbs and is some twelve to fourteen inches long, carrying a dozen or more coconut-scented carmine and pink flowers. This species does well in a fairly big teak basket and requires ample warmth and moisture when growing, with a distinct rest afterwards to ripen the bulbs. Water must be kept from the young growths. This orchid is well worth growing.

D. Mac Carthiæ (Wesak mal.)

A very handsome orchid, endemic in Ceylon and found only in the Ratnapura district. Pseudo-bulbs, thin and pendent, purplish-grey. Leaves, grassy and deciduous. Flowers, large, slightly fragrant, produced in May in pairs from the nodes of the ripened pseudo-bulbs. They are beautifully coloured, sepals and petals rosy-purple, lip-lavender-netted with purple, has a large white blotch in the front lobe and a blotch of deep purple in the throat. This is not an easily-grown orchid. It requires very little compost, and is best accommodated in baskets. It needs a hot, steamy atmosphere with a decided period of rest after the growing season. If this plant is not protected it will soon be non-existent, for masses of it are torn ruthlessly and bodily from the jungles annually for the sake of its flowers.

DENDROBIUM LYONI
Single flower (Natural Size)

DENDROBIUM NOBILE

D. macrophyllum

A large-growing species from New Guinea. Pseudo-bulbs, eight to twelve inches high, quill-like at base, then thickening to the apex, two-leaved. Flower-spike, apical, produced in June or July; twelve inches long, many-flowered. Flowers about two inches in diameter, yellow and white; lip, yellow, blotched with purple. Whole flower is edged and backed with hairs.

D. macrostachyum

Another, but common, Ceylon orchid, found all over the low-country. Pseudo-bulbs much as in *D. Mac Carthiæ*. Flowers, small, greenish-yellow netted with purple. Lip, small. They are borne in profusion during spring and summer.

D. nobile

A well-known and very beautiful orchid from India, Burma, etc. Pseudo-bulbs one foot or more high; evergreen. The flowers are borne in twos or threes in early summer from the nodes of the mature (leafy) pseudo-bulbs. They are long-lasting and fragrant, pure white, tipped with amethyst. Lip, large and spreading, blotched with deep purple. This is one of the most well-known, and it is certainly one of the most beautiful orchids grown. It will thrive under much cooler conditions than most of the genus, and is extremely difficult to flower at the low elevations. There are several varieties of this species.

D. Parishii

A very pretty, small-growing plant from Burma. Pseudo-bulbs, one foot long, semi-erect, thick and fleshy. Leaves deciduous. The flowers are borne in clusters of three in early spring from the nodes of the ripened pseudo-bulbs. They are of a beautiful rosy-purple; the lip being deep purple and acute-pointed.

D. Phalænopsis

An exceptionally fine orchid from Java, Australia and New Guinea. Pseudo-bulbs, one foot high, grey, slightly swollen in the middle, erect and woody. Leaves, lanceolate, persistent for a considerable time. The flower spike is produced in summer from the apices of the mature pseudo-bulbs. It is erect and many-flowered. The latter are about two and a half inches across, and are rather like *Phalænopsis* in shape. They may be either deep purple or white, with many of the intermediate shades. They are long-lasting and very beautiful and some of the forms resemble an everlasting or sweet pea. They require a little more shading than the rest and need a hot, steamy atmosphere, and should never be severely rested. The new growths are produced about six to eight months after the flowering period.

D. Pierardi

A fairly common but very pretty Indian species. Pseudo-bulbs, pendent, two to four feet long, clothed with lanceolate, deciduous leaves. It is an easily cultivated and very free-flowering species. The latter are produced in great profusion from the nodes of the mature (leafless) pseudo-bulbs in spring or summer, in pairs. They are about two inches across, sepals and petals, pale lilac-mauve, the lip being tubular, velvety, pale-yellow, veined with purple in the throat. The margin is very slightly fringed.

D. primulinum

A pretty and free-flowering species from Burma. Pseudo-bulbs, semi-erect, greenish-yellow. Leaves, deciduous. The flowers are produced in pairs from the nodes of the mature pseudo-bulbs in spring. They are two and a half inches in diameter, pale lilac. Lip, pale yellow. The whole flower has a "frosty" appearance, being covered with fine silky hairs.

D. Regium

A very handsome, summer-flowering orchid from India. Pseudo-bulbs much as those of *D. nobile.* The large flowers are borne in axillary racemes of two, or more. They are deep crimson-magenta, and last a long time in full beauty if not wetted.

D. superbum

A beautiful species from Java and New Guinea. Pseudo-bulbs long and drooping, greyish-purple, leaves lanceolate, deciduous. The flowers are borne in pairs from the nodes of the mature growths in winter. They are very large, and of a deep rosy-purple. Lip, large, scoop-shaped, beautifully shaded with purple and crimson.

DENDROBIUM REGIUM

To face page 64

Photo by J. E. Baillie-Hamilton, Esq.

DENDROBIUM THYRSIFLORUM

To face page 65

They have a strong rhubarb-like scent. Flowers often four inches or more across.

D. thyrsiflorum

An evergreen, very handsome orchid from India and Burma. Pseudo-bulbs, growth, etc., almost exactly as in *D. densiflorum*, except that the pseudo-bulbs are shorter and greenish instead of brown in *D. densiflorum Schroderianum.* The flowers however are creamy-white, while the large, downy lip is deep yellow. It is an exceptionally showy and free-flowering orchid, and produces its masses of flowers in spring. The flowers are fragrant.

D. tortile rosea

A pretty species from Burma. Pseudo-bulbs, one foot or more high, erect, club-shaped, "jointed," yellow when mature. Leaves, deciduous. The flowers are produced in profusion from the nodes of the mature pseudo-bulbs, in pairs, in the early months of the year. They are some three inches in diameter. Sepals and petals pale lilac-rose, curiously twisted. Lip, large, yellow, with a blotch of purple in the throat.

D. transparens

An Indian and Burmese species, very similar in growth and appearance to *D. Pierardi*. The flowers are produced in pairs from the nodes of the ripened pseudo-bulbs. They are medium-sized, pale pink, tipped with amethyst. Lip, white with a couple of purple blotches in the front lobe, and tipped with amethyst.

D. Wardianum

A beautiful and free-flowering species from Burma. Pseudo-bulbs, semi-erect, two to three feet long, stout, nodes much thickened (as in *D. crassinode*), greyish-brown when mature. Leaves deciduous, three inches long, blunt and lanceolate. The large flowers (three to four inches across) are borne in profusion in twos or threes from the nodes of the ripened pseudo-bulbs in spring. They are creamy-white and waxy, sepals and petals tipped with rose-purple. Lip, large and spreading, white, with two purple blotches on the front lobe and a large blotch of yellow in the throat. This is one of the best of the whole family, the flowers are very long-lasting and showy.

Among other species are:—*D. atro-violaceum*, *D. denudans*. *D. Brymerianum*, *D. lassioglossum*, *D. speciosum*, *D. superbiens*, (both Australian), *D. spec:* (Java), *D. Victoria Regina* (a rare " blue " Dendrobe from New Guinea) and many others.

DENDROCHILUM

A small family of epiphytal orchids referred to as *Platyclinis* (which see).

DOVE ORCHIDS (See Peristeria)

EPI-CATTLEYA

A bigeneric family derived by intercrossing *Cattleyas* with some of the *Epidendrums*.

The plants and flowers (often very handsome) are intermediate, and may be given the same treatment as advised for *Cattleyas*.

EPI-CATT-LÆLIA

A small group of orchids derived from intercrossing three families, *Epidendrum*, *Cattleya*, and *Lælia*. They are very interesting and should be treated as *Cattleyas*.

EPIDENDRUM

A fairly large family of tropical epiphytal orchids, natives of South America. Their generic name points to the fact that they are epiphytes. They are however, not much cultivated, the two species described here, being perhaps the only species that are much in evidence. They may be grown in pots or baskets in an ordinary compost, and enjoy plenty of water, sun and air when growing.

E. radicans

A slender-growing, trailing plant ; may be grown up a trellis, etc. Pseudo-bulbs, slender, climbing, white roots being produced from all parts of it. Flowers very showy, borne in a terminal cluster on a short spike. They are brilliant scarlet and orange, individually small, but produced in mass and very showy.

E. Wallisii

May be grown in pots as for *Arundina bambusifolia* (which it much resembles in growth, habit, etc.) Pseudo-bulbs three feet high. The flowers are borne in terminal clusters and are about two inches in diameter; deep yellow, blotched with crimson. Lip, white, veined with crimson, fragrant.

This species requires plenty of water and rooting space when growing.

Other species include :—*E. vitellinum, E. atro-purpureum*, etc., and very many are worthy of places for their quaint, often showy flowers.

EPI-PHRONITIS

An interesting family obtained from intercrossing *Epidendrums* with *Sophronitis* (usually *Grandiflora.*)

Cultural requirements are intermediate and they will often succeed in conditions slightly warmer than those advised for *Sophronitis.*

ERIA

A fairly large family of epiphytes, natives of tropical Asia.

They are not largely cultivated, but one or two of them are quite pretty.

They prefer basket treatment with plenty of water when growing, and are best managed in fairly cool, shaded positions.

E. bicolor

Ceylon, 4,000 feet (Lily of the Valley Orchid). This is a common, pretty little orchid, well known in Ceylon. Pseudobulbs thick and fleshy, four inches high, as thick as the little finger and of a purplish-brown colour. The two or three leaves are apical, acute-pointed and strap-shaped, four to eight inches long.

Raceme erect, many-flowered, deep purple, produced in spring and summer. Flowers bell-shaped, pure white, very like a lily of the valley. Bracts reddish-purple. A well-flowered plant is very pretty.

E. braccata

Another Ceylon orchid, 3,500 feet. Pseudo-bulbs one inch in diameter, crowded and flattened, two-leaved.

The flower scape is slender, two inches long, one-flowered, produced in winter. The flowers are large for the size of the plant. They are fragrant, pure white with a yellow stain inside the lip; in shape very like a *Cœlogyne.*

E. coronaria. (*Trichosma suavis.*)

Northern India. Pseudo-bulbs three inches high, fleshy; leaves apical, two deep green, broad.

The flower-spike is produced from the apex of the pseudo-bulbs in winter: erect, many-flowered.

They are of medium size, pure white, with a little crimson, brown and yellow on the large trilobed lip. Fragrant.

EULOPHIA.

A fairly small family of showy-flowered terrestrial orchids, natives of tropical Asia. They are pseudo-bulbous, and have a creeping rhizome from which the compressed pseudo-bulb is produced.

Leaves, two feet long, erect and plaited, or thin and grass-like. Flower-scape erect, produced with the new growths, many-flowered. They require to be grown in pots in a shaded, moist and warm position.

After flowering they should be rested for a month or two. Leaf mould, some loam and fine sand will suit them well, provided the drainage is good.

About five species are known and they are not much cultivated, though some of them are well worth cultivation on account of their long-lasting nature.

E. macrostachya

Native of Ceylon (2,000 feet). Flowers medium-sized, greenish-yellow, flushed with rose; lip elongated and drooping, bright yellow, borne in summer.

E. Guineensis

A large grower, flowers green, shaded with deep purple, lip white. Spike erect, three feet high and many-flowered.

E. (unidentified).

A large-growing, free-flowering kind from Burma. Flower spikes over three feet high, bearing many long-lasting purplish-rose flowers, which are about one and a half inches in depth. Lip large and toothed; front lobe serrated. This species flowers from March to July.

E. virens

A native of Ceylon (low country). It is not such a strong grower as the last; Flowers greenish-yellow, lip large, white veined with red.

GEODORUM

A small family of tuberous-rooted terrestrial orchids from Burma and Malaysia; they will succeed under the same conditions as are afforded to *Eulophia*.

G. candidum.

Leaves, six inches long, plaited, deep green, short-stemmed, oval. Spike, erect, eight inches high, bearing a bunch of bell-shaped, white flowers, which are beautifully flushed with rose. The small enclosed lip is stained with yellow.

The flowers are produced in late summer.

GONGORA

A smallish family of pseudo-bulbous epiphytes from South America, well suited to basket culture and treated as advised for *Stanhopeas.*

Flowers on a pendent or drooping raceme—often carrying over twenty blooms. They are variable in colour, yellow and brown being most predominant. Labellum often inverted and grotesquely-shaped.

The flowers are often very fragrant. The only member of the family I possess at the moment is:—

G. galeata.

South America: pseudo-bulbs two inches high, round, diphyllous. Raceme, ten-and fifteen-flowered, blooms in January to March. Flowers, pale pink, spotted with brown. Lip, shiny yellow. Fragrant.

GRAMMANGIS

A small family from Madagascar, allied to *Grammatophyllum* (which see for culture, etc.)

G. Ellisii.

This is the only member of the family that is usually procurable, and is sometimes known as *Grammatophyllum Ellisii.*

Pseudo-bulbs one foot high, quadrangular. Leaves, oblong-ovate, eighteen inches or more long. The scape is borne in summer from the bases of the new pseudo-bulbs; it is many-flowered. The blooms are large and showy, orange-yellow, streaked with reddish-brown. Lip, white, flushed with pale rose.

GRAMMATOPHYLLUM

A fairly large family of terrestorial and epiphytal orchids from the warmer and moister parts of Madagascar, Africa, and the East Indies.

They are not widely-cultivated orchids, but as one of them is the giant of the orchid family, mention of it must be made. The whole family requires plenty of heat and sunlight; a good open compost and copious supplies of water during the growing season.

G. Fenzlianum.

Native of Malacca. Pseudo-bulbs, six inches high, bearing lanceolate leaves which often exceed eighteen inches in length. Scapes, many-flowered; three feet long. The flowers are fairly large, pale greenish-yellow spotted with brown. The lip is large, pale yellow striped with brown.

G. Rumphianum.

Native of Malaysia. Pseudo-bulbs, eight inches long. The blooms are of a fair size, pale ochre-yellow, thickly spotted with brown. Lip, yellow, striped and spotted with brown and veined with purple.

G. speciosum.

A very large-growing, sturdy plant, native of Malacca and Java. Pseudo-bulbs erect, eight or nine feet high, four to six inches in diameter, clothed with strap-shaped, glossy, drooping leaves, one foot or more long.

The spikes are many-flowered, erect, terminal, produced in autumn. The flowers are large, yellow, blotched with purple. This is about the largest known orchid.

HABENARIA

A large family of terrestrial, tuberous-rooted orchids.

They are seldom cultivated, though some of them are well worth growing.

They require to be well drained and given a light open compost containing some good loam.

They must be given plenty of water during the growing season with a prolonged rest afterwards.

H. plantaginea.

Native of Ceylon. Leaves, oblong-ovate, radical, some eight inches in length. Scape, erect, bearing a few large pure white flowers. The lip is much serrated and ends in a long spur.

H. pterocarpa.

Another Ceylon orchid (3,000 feet). Leaves radical—produced in a sort of rosette on the ground, four inches long, broad and pale green.

Spike, erect, borne in summer. Flowers, about six in number, pure white, very much frilled and toothed.

Lip, large for the size of the flower, serrated. Spur, one and a half inches long, pale greenish-white.

H. Susannæ.

A large-flowered and showy species from India, etc. The flowers are pure white, and the lip is beautifully fringed and serrated.

Other species include:—*H. militaris*, *H. pusillæ*, etc. During the resting season this genus should only be given sufficient water to maintain the plumpness of the tubers.

H. Pusillæ is a pink-flowering species and is deserving of a place in every collection.

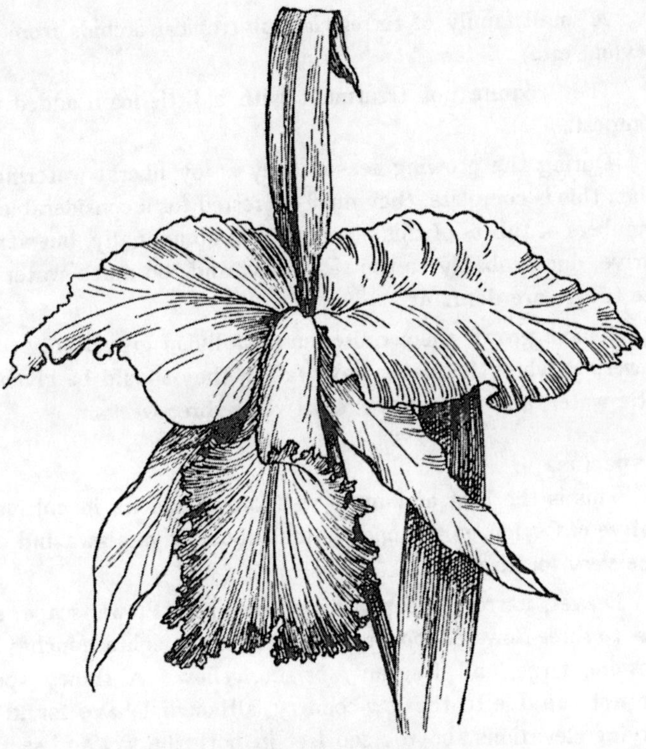

LÆLIO-CATTLEYA "ERICA SANDER"
Variety (Very much reduced.)

IPSEA

A small family of terrestrial sub-tropical orchids from India, Ceylon, etc.

They require pot treatment with a little loam added to the compost.

During the growing season they enjoy liberal watering, but when this is complete, they must be rested for a considerable time. Numbers of tubers of this plant arc dug up annually, but very few thrive; due probably to too rich a soil and too much water when the tubers are dormant.

I have grown them quite successfully in gravel only. After flowering, when the leaves have fallen, they should be given very little water, and that once every two or three weeks.

I. speciosa.

This is the best and most well-known species in cultivation. Native of Ceylon, in the open patnas about Diyatalawa and otherwise very localised.

Leaves, narrow and plaited, sword-like. Flower-scape, erect, one- to three-flowered, borne in early summer, eighteen inches high. Flowers, large and fragrant, bright yellow. A showy species, but not suitable to the low-country, although I have found it at varying elevations above 1,200 feet in both the wet and semi-dry zones.

LÆLIA

An exceptionally showy family of epiphytal South American orchids. They are very similar in growth, habit and appearance to *Cattleyas*, and thrive under the same treatment. They require plenty of sunlight and air during the growing season and careful syringing in hot weather is most beneficial; though care must be taken to prevent water lodging in the new growths and scape sheathes.

Leaves usually solitary, sometimes in pairs.

Flowers are borne in erect scapes of three or four from the apices of the ripened pseudo-bulbs.

They are best suited to elevations of 2,000 to 5,000 feet and need a thorough resting when growth is complete.

Their name is legion, but as they are not much cultivated in Ceylon mention need only be made of one of the finest in the species.

L. anceps.

Pseudo-bulb three inches high, oval and slightly furrowed, one-leaved. The flower scape is long, arching, and flattened: bears four or five large flowers in winter.

The flowers are some three to four inches in diameter and of a beautiful rosy-purple colour. The large open lip is deep purple with crimson shadings, the throat being deep yellow streaked with rich purple. There are very many colour variations of this orchid, varying from white to deep rose.

Other species include the following beautiful orchids:—*L. grandis*, *L. purpurata*, etc., and many very beautiful hybrids have been derived from intercrossing with *Cattleyas*, *Brassavolas* and *Sophronitis*.

LÆLIO-CATTLEYA

This is the name given to hybrids derived from the cross-fertilization of *Cattleyas* with *Lælias*. There are several hundreds in cultivation and more are produced annually. They require

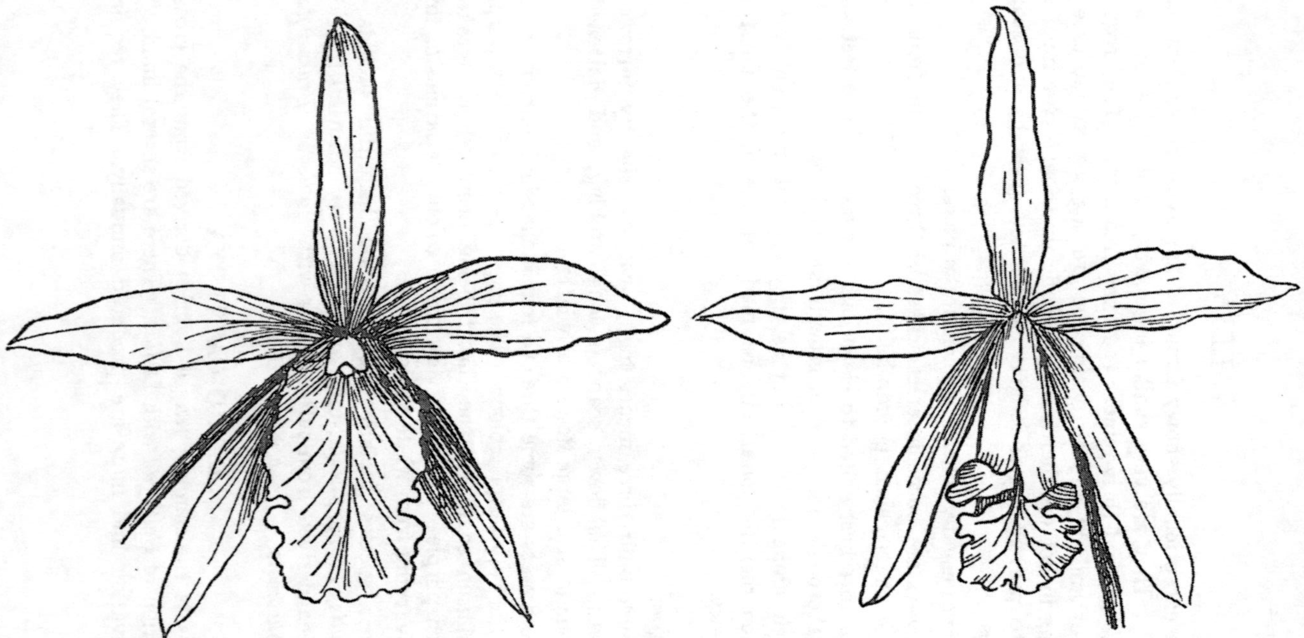

Open lip

Closed lip

LÆLIO—CATTLEYA. G. S. BALL

Two varieties on same spike (Reduced)

much the same treatment as *Cattleyas;* are usually hardy, and easily managed, while the flowers are often superb.

Members of this hybrid family are being imported into Ceylon and the East generally, in annually increasing numbers and are not a little responsible for the growing interest in Orchid Culture. A selection from any trade catalogue will prove interesting and extremely beautiful.

LIPARIS

A large family of epiphytal tropical orchids from Asia.

Flowers poor, usually dull greenish-white, borne on an erect, many-flowered scape from the apices of the mature pseudo-bulbs.

L. longipes.

Native of Ceylon, (2,000 feet pseudo-bulbs fleshy, oblong-ovate, pale-green, three inches long, two-leaved. Leaves, stalked, spathulate. Scape many-flowered, produced in spring. Flowers, greenish-white, small.

L. Wightiana.

Ceylon, (4,000 feet) pseudo-bulbs oval, fleshy, two-leaved, brownish-purple. Scape, erect, many-flowered, produced in summer. Flowers small, pale greenish-yellow. Both the above may be cultivated in baskets in moss and must be kept damp and shaded.

LYCASTE

A large-flowered and handsome family of epiphytal orchids from South America.

They are not suited to elevations under 3,000 feet, but I have grown them to perfection at 5,000 feet. They require basket or pot treatment in an ordinary compost with plenty of finely-broken crocks and charcoal.

They must be given plenty of water during the growing season and should never be severely rested. Watering must at all times be carefully attended to, and the compost must never get sour.

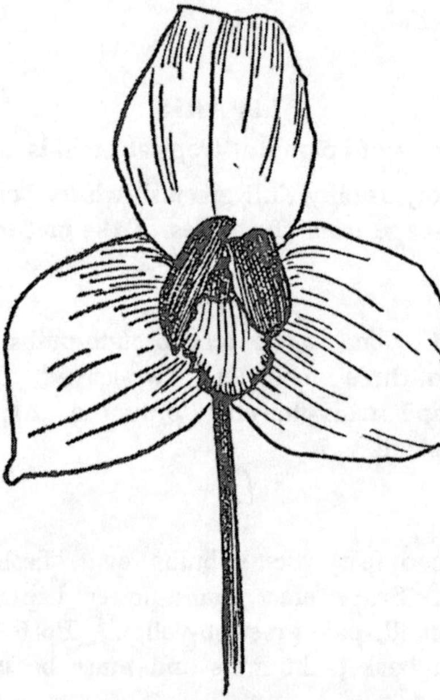

LYCASTE SKINNERI (Variety).

L. Skinneri.

This is about the best in the genus. Pseudo-bulbs, swollen, three inches high, two-leaved. Leaves dark-green, deep nerved and glossy.

The erect scape is one-flowered and several are produced in autumn from the base of the new pseudo-bulbs. Flowers, some three and a half inches in diameter, bluish-white or rosy-purple, very variable. The large lip is white, profusely dotted with crimson. Other fine species include:—*L. Deppei*, *L. macrcphylla*, etc., and the whole family is well worth cultivating at the higher elevations, indeed it is surprising that more of this family are not grown Up-country, as they are easy to manage, usually bloom profusely and are very showy.

LAELIO-CATTLEYA "MARTINETTI"
Variety (Reduced)

MICROSTYLIS

A small genus of terrestrial orchids, natives of India, Ceylon, etc. They require the same treatment as advised for *Anœctochilus*, and are cultivated for the sake of their succulent, coloured leaves.

M. discolor.

Native of Ceylon (at all elevations). Stems pseudo-bulbous, three to six inches high, purplish red. Leaves, oblong-ovate, some five inches long, deeply ribbed. They are of a uniform deep purplish red. Flowers small. In other species the leaves vary from bright green to green and brown.

MILTONIA

A large and very beautiful family of epiphytal tropical South American orchids, very nearly allied to *Odontoglossum*, and requiring the same treatment. One of the best of the species, however, *M. Rœzlii*, can be cultivated with great success in warm positions, while very many can be induced to bloom at medium elevations, and deserve much more attention than they now get. This genus is peculiar in that many of members have leaves of a light yellowish, or greyish green. This must not be taken as a sign of ill-health, and the plants over-watered, or over-shaded, which would be fatal.

They all require care and attention, a little light, open compost and careful watering and shading. They will not stand drought, strong sunlight, nor water lying in the centres of the young growth—nor yet perpetually wet feet. During the dull months of the year—when root-growth is inactive—they should be given very little water.

M. Rœzlii.

A native of Colombia. Pseudo-bulbs oval, crowded, some two inches high, bearing two apical and one apical leaves, which are about ten inches long, thin, and narrow. The erect scapes are produced in early spring and bear (usually) three large flowers which are shaped like a pansy. Sepals and petals pure white, the petals having a purple basal blotch. Lip, large, pure white, shaded with purple and yellow. This is a very fine orchid and one ithat repays care. It often blooms twice in the year. Others nclude:—*M. candida, M. spectabilis, M. vexillaria*, etc., several of which are very showy, and there are now numerous beautiful hybrids, which certainly should receive a great deal more attention.

ODONTOGLOSSUM

Although this is a cool-climate genus and, with one or two exceptions, can only be cultivated at elevations of 5,000 feet to 6,000 feet, mention of it must be made here, as it has produced some of the very finest orchids now in cultivation.

They are a large family and are natives of the mountainous parts of Central and South America.

Surely everyone at home knows the lovely *O. crispum* with its masses of lovely pure white, brown-blotched, very much crisped flowers; it is one of the most useful and graceful orchids in existence. For the use of collectors at the higher elevations, a few hints on its culture may be of advantage.

I have grown it quite successfully at an elevation of 5,000 feet, out of doors, slightly shaded from the hot mid-day sun. An excellent compost is made of bracken-roots, charcoal, moss and decayed oak leaves (if one is fortunate enough to possess one of these trees), failing this, a mixture of chopped moss, fine charcoal, fern roots (killed by immersion in boiling water), will serve the turn.

The compost should be well-drained and raised slightly above the level of the pot.

The rhizome and pseudo-bulbs should be made to sit firmly on the top of the mound.

When the new pseudo-bulbs and flower spikes are forming, water should be given copiously and at no time should they be allowed to become very dry. During the resting season they should be placed in lighter and airier positions, and at all times they enjoy plenty of fresh air, and the damper the latter is, the better.

O. crispum.

Pseudo-bulbs, three inches high, oval and fleshy, bearing two apical, narrow, leathery leaves some ten inches in length. The long, arching and sometimes branched flower scape is produced from near the base of the new pseudo-bulbs at different seasons. Flowers, two and a half inches in diameter, pure glistening white, very much crisped at the edges. The large lip is curiously "toothed" and is clear yellow spotted with irregular blotches of dull red.

There must be nearly one hundred and fifty species of *Odontoglossum* and as many hybrids, and they are all beautiful.

Other well-known species are:—*O. grande, O. maculatum, O. maxillare, O. nobile, O. triumphans,* etc.

O. grande and its allies may be grown with the *Cattleyas,* and are well worth a place.

ONCIDIUM

This is another large genus of epiphytal orchids, natives of America. They are more suited to culture in warm climates than *Odontoglots* and some of them are quite as showy and free-flowering, although the flowers are not, as a rule, so large individually.

They require the same treatment and compost as *Odontoglots* (to which they are allied), but may be grown easily at all elevations in Ceylon (with the exception of a few cool species and *O. papilio,* which requires a hot, moist climate).

Very little compost is needed and they must not be dried to any extent ; though a reduced supply of water is needed in the resting season with a light and airy position.

O. ampliatum.

A large-growing and free-flowering species. Pseudo-bulbs large, compressed and semi-spherical, deep green, spotted dull mauve, becoming greyish-brown when old. The leaves are strap-shaped, deep green and leathery, ten inches long. The strong, arching and often branched, many-flowered raceme is produced in spring from the bases of the ripened pseudo-bulbs.

The flowers are about two inches in diameter. Sepals and petals smallish, pale yellow, dotted with reddish-brown, while the large lip is of the same colour.

O. Kramerianum.

Very similar to *O. papilio* in requirements and growth of flowers.

O. macranthum.

A very showy and strong-growing orchid. Pseudo-bulbs, three inches high, oblong, flattened and slightly furrowed, springing from a creeping rhizome.

Leaves strap-shaped, recurved, one foot long, leathery and acute-pointed. Flower scape produced from the leaf-sheathes in summer from the young ripened pseudo-bulbs.

It is six to eight feet long, semi-erect and sometimes branching, many-flowered. The latter are three or four inches in diameter. The whole flower is of a golden yellow colour, lip small, deep purple, with a white ridge in the centre of the front lobe.

O. papilio.

The well-known "Butterfly Orchid" from the West Indies. Pseudo-bulbs round, furrowed and very closely set, each bearing a solitary deep green, leathery leaf, eight inches long, which is blotched with brown.

Flower scape long, arching and slightly flattened, bearing a single large flower. It is produced from the base of the ripened pseudo-bulbs at various seasons of the year.

The flowers are large and very curiously shaped. Sepals erect, purplish-brown, narrow, three inches high.

The two side petals are reflexed, two inches long, deep yellow, irregularly blotched with reddish-brown, lip, large and "frilled," yellow blotched with brown.

This species require plenty of sunlight and a hot, moist atmosphere when growing.

After the first flower has faded the scape should not be cut off, as others will be developed soon after the first has faded and there is very often a succession of four or five flowers on the same scape, but if the plant becomes weak, it is as well to remove all the flower scapes and encourage new growth.

O. varicosum.

Another showy and free-flowering plant that bears quantities of brightly-coloured flowers in autumn. Pseudo-bulbs oblong, three inches high, furrowed and swollen, bearing two apical and two lateral stiff, recurved, dark green leaves, eight inches long.

Flower spikes semi-erect, branching, six feet or more in length, produced in autumn from the bases of the ripened pseudo-bulbs.

Flowers one and a half inches in diameter. Sepals and petals small, " frilled," pale greenish yellow, blotched with brown. Lip, very large and spreading, deep yellow and of a peculiar kidney-like shape.

There are many other very fine species among this genus:—*O. crispum, O. Lanceanum, O. Marshallianum, O. splendidum*, etc.

O. Lanceanum will flourish under conditions suitable to *O. papilio.*

PACHYSTOMA

This is another name for the family Ipsea (q.v.)

PAPHINIA

A small family of epiphytal tropical South American orchids. They are best cultivated in shallow pots (well-drained) in a mixture of shredded bracken roots, good loam and broken charcoal. During the growing season they should be given plenty of water and though they do not need to be severely rested, a reduced amount of water should be given when at rest. They require constant shading.

P. cristata.

A very handsome species bearing large yellow flowers which are blotched with purplish brown. The lip bears a tuft of hairs. The flowers often exceed four inches in diameter.

Another species is *P. grandiflora.*

PERISTERIA

This is the name for the well-known "Dove Orchids," so called from the resemblance the column and side lobes of the lip bears to a dove with its wings spread. They are naturally epiphytal and are natives of Central and South America. It is usual however to treat them as terrestrial orchids, as their needs seem easier to supply when grown as such.

They should be well-drained and given a rich compost of decayed leaves, good soil, charcoal, a few pieces of broken, decayed bones and a little clean sand.

During the growing season they must have copious supplies of water and when the flower spikes are appearing in early summer, a little liquid manure may be given with advantage once a week. They enjoy a warm and shady position.

P. elata.

Pseudo-bulbs, large and rounded, three inches, or more high bearing three or four long-pointed, plaited leaves one foot or more in length.

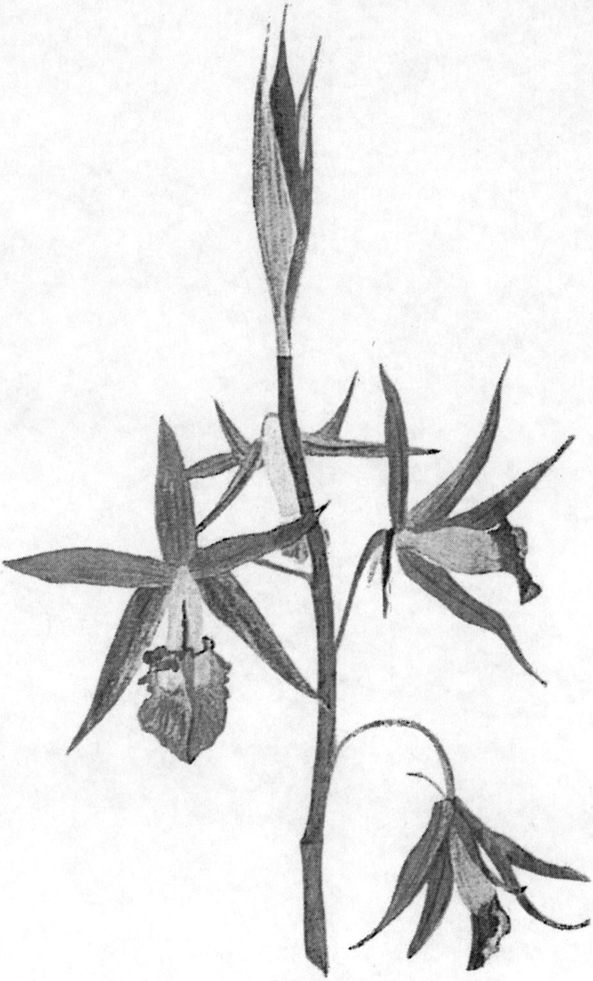

PHAIUS BICOLOR

To face page 87

Flower spike erect, many-flowered, produced in summer from the base of the mature pseudo-bulbs, two to three feet high.

Flowers fairly "cupped" and large waxy, fragrant and long-lasting, pure white. The column is very like a bird's head and being attached to the side-lobes of the lip, which provides the wings, very much resembles a dove with wings outspread.

The column and side lobes of the lip are thickly spotted with purple.

This orchid is commonly known as the "Holy Ghost Orchid." When growth is complete they should be rested. Other species include:—*P. cerina* and *P. pendula*, both of which should be grown in baskets as advised for *Stanhopeas*.

PHAIUS

A very useful, showy-flowered and handsome genus of tropical epiphytal and terrestrial orchids.

They are large and ornamental growers and even when not in flower are useful on account of their crop of handsome, dark green, "ribbed" leaves.

They are not difficult to grow and will succeed under the same treatment as is given to the evergreen *Calanthes*.

The pseudo-bulbs are large, rounded and knotted, springing from a creeping rhizome and are often themselves underground.

They should have liberal treatment in the growing season with a rest when growth is complete. When, however, the flower spikes appear they may be given a little liquid manure with advantage, say once a week.

P. bicolor.

A handsome large-growing species, native of Ceylon (2,000 to 5,000 feet, on the edges of jungles and in open patnas.

Pseudo-bulbs knotted and creeping on a stout rhizome. Leaves, tall, erect and deep-nerved, two to four feet high. Flower spike erect, three feet high, produced from the bases of the mature pseudo-bulbs in spring and summer; many-flowered.

The latter are some two and a half to four inches across. Sepals and petals lance-shaped, reddish-brown; lip, large and spreading, tongue-shaped, yellow or white, flushed with crimson, the side lobes being rose-crimson. The flowers are very variable in colour and size, dependent largely upon shade and treatment. There is a very handsome variety of this in which the whole flower is of a soft lemon yellow.

P. Blumei.

A native of Java. Pseudo-bulbs much as in *P. bicolor,* but rounder. Leaves similar but shorter and broader.

Flower scape erect, produced in spring from the bases of the mature pseudo-bulbs, two to three feet high and many-flowered.

The flowers are large and showy. Sepals and petals lanceolate, brownish-yellow. The lip, is large and acute-pointed, crimson margined with pale-yellow.

P. luridus.

Native of Ceylon (low-country), endemic, rather rare. Pseudo-bulbs much as in *P. bicolor* but not so large. Stems two to three feet high, quadrangular, leaves broad and ribbed, eighteen inches long, pointed, borne from the stem. The flower spike is produced in autumn from the sheathing bases of the leaves. It is erect, some two feet high, and many-flowered. The flowers are about one and a half inches in diameter, pale yellow striped longitudinally with red, sepals and petals acute-pointed. Lip, small, clear yellow.

P. maculatus.

Native of Northern India. Pseudo-bulbs ovate and knotted, two inches high. Leaves broad, lanceolate, two feet long, deep green spotted with white. Spike erect, produced from the bases of the newly-formed pseudo-bulbs, two feet high, bearing about eight large yellow flowers. Lip tubular, clear yellow, the middle lobe being streaked with brown.

P. simulans.

Native of Madagascar. Not of easy culture but is well worth attempting for its very beautiful flowers. Pseudo-bulbs slender, borne at intervals on the creeping rhizome. Leaves, acute-pointed, ribbed, some ten inches in length. The basal flower spike is erect and is borne from the bases of the newly formed pseudo-bulbs

Flowers are fairly large, sepals and petals pure white while the large and very handsome lip is trilobed, the side lobes being pale yellow in which the colour is almost obliterated by the thick spotting of dull crimson. The front lobe is crisped at the margin, white, spotted with rich purple. This species should be treated almost as an epiphyte and needs no soil in its compost, usually a little moss fastened about its roots being sufficient, provided the plant is kept moist and shaded. It enjoys a high temperature, and need not be severely rested. Epiphyte.

P. Wallichii.

A fine large-growing plant, native of Assam and Nepal. Pseudo-bulbs very similar to those of *P. grandifolias.* Flowers large, reddish-buff flushed with crimson. Lip, yellow and white. Reverse side of flowers dull white.

PHALÆNOPSIS

A medium-sized family of strikingly beautiful evergreen epiphytal orchids, natives of the tropical parts of the old world. The name is a good one and is very descriptive:—Phalaina, i.e., a moth; opsis, i.e., like (Greek).

They are non-pseudo-bulbous and the thick, fleshy roots are produced in profusion.

Leaves, tongue-shaped or oval, leathery. The plants are best grown in baskets in a hot, moist position (away from the sun's rays) in a compost of chopped moss and fine charcoal, or gravel.

Flowers are very large and showy and exceptionally long-lasting. They are produced in quantity and are very gracefully set on the arching racemes.

They are not the easiest orchids to cultivate successfully, but are well worth the extra care that can be given them. Drips and draughts are fatal.

P. amabilis.

A truly beautiful orchid, native of Java and the Philippine Islands.

Leaves, deep green, eight inches long by three inches wide, leathery and oval. Raceme, semi-erect, many-flowered, produced in summer and autumn from the " crown " of the plant. Flowers very large, often four and a half inches or more across; pure white.

Sepals are broader than the petals, very symmetrical. The tri-lobed lip is white, stained with yellow and faintly spotted with purplish-red. The front lobe is curiously elongated at the apex into two thread-like tails about one and a half inches long.

P. Aphrodite.

A large-leaved plant from the Philippine Islands. Leaves, like those of *amabilis*, dull purple on reverse side.

Flowers, borne in autumn on a long, arching spray. They are large and pure white; very handsome. The lip is flushed with yellow and has several blotches of purple. The front lobe is of the same formation as *P. amabilis.*

P. Denevei.

A curious *Vanda*-like plant from Borneo, scarce and quaint. The leaves are very similar to those of *Vanda Kimballiana*. The flower scape is borne in spring and summer from the axils of the leaves and carries from four to eight blossoms. They are yellow, of good size and substance, and are profusely spotted with brown-purple. The short lip is spreading, purple, fading to yellow in the throat.

P. Denevei alba is the white variety of this orchid and is a very fine plant.

P. Lowii.

A small, though very pretty little plant from Lower Burma, etc. Leaves, purplish-green, strap-shaped, thick and pointed, four inches long. The erect spike is borne during summer and bears about fifteen flowers, which are nearly two inches across. Sepals and petals, white, tinged with purple; lip, tri-lobed, the middle lobe being deep purple while the side lobes are paler. Column, pale purple. Rather hard to manage with any success.

P. Luddemanniana.

A handsome plant from the Philippine Islands. Leaves thick and leathery, oblong-ovate, some eight inches in length. The flower spike is short and sturdy, bearing a few large flowers in summer. The sepals and petals are white, beautifully banded with purple at the bases, which merges into brown at the apices. Lip, rich purple.

PHALÆNOPSIS DENEVEI

To face page 90

P. Parishii.

A small, but pretty *Phalænopsis* from Burma. Leaves, three to four inches long by two and a half inches wide; deep-green. Flower scape as long as the leaves, four to eight-flowered, produced in spring and summer. The flowers are about one and a half inches in diameter, pure white. The centre lobe of the trilobed lip is rosy-mauve with a yellow centre and white crest. Side lobes yellow, small, spotted with purple.

P. Sanderiana.

Native of the Philippine Islands. Leaves very similar to those of *P. Schilleriana*, but shorter. The strong spike bears a quantity of large flowers (chiefly in the summer) which often attain a width of four inches, and are of a beautiful rosy-mauve colour. The tri-lobed lip is white, the side lobes being slightly spotted with purple, while the front lobe is flushed with yellow and has two long, apical filaments—much as in *P. amabilis*.

P. Schilleriana.

Another exceedingly beautiful orchid from the Philippine Islands. Leaves, oval, long and broad, dark green, mottled, and blotched with dull white; very handsome, presenting a marbled appearance. They are thick and leathery; purple underneath.

Flower spike long, arching, many-flowered and sometimes branching, borne in the summer months from the " crown " of the plant. The blossoms are some three inches across and are of lovely pinkish-rose colour, bordered with white. The tri-lobed lip is pink or white, while the front lobe is divided into two short filaments. It has a blotch of yellow at the base, spotted with dull red. There is beautiful white variety of this, *P. Schilleriana Alba*.

P. Stuartiana.

A very fine orchid from the Philippine Islands. Leaves, large, mottled with grey as in *P. Schilleriana*, dull purple on the reverse. Flower scape long and arching, bearing several fairly large flowers; mainly white and yellow, spotted with purple. The centre lobe of the lip has two cordate filaments.

P. violacea.

A very long-lasting and fragrant orchid from Java. Leaves, rounded, thick and leathery, deep green, about five inches long by four inches broad.

The flower scape is short (about five inches) and bears a succession of long-lasting flowers from April to August. They are about two and a half inches across. Petals and sepals pointed, broad, deep, rosy-purple, fading at the apices to yellowish-green. Lip deep purple with some orange at the base. I have had a couple of these plants in flower for several months.

Other beautiful species are:—*P. leucorrhoda*, *P. speciosa*, *P. cornu-cervi*, *P. Mannii*, *P. modesta*, etc.

PHOLIDOTA

A small family of tropical epiphytal orchids, natives of Ceylon and India. They require basket treatment, but are not commonly cultivated.

P. imbricata.

A native of Ceylon (apparently at all elevations). Pseudobulbs three inches long, swollen and furrowed, deep green, bearing one apical, nerved leaf one foot long on a stalk of about three inches.

Raceme, many-flowered, produced in summer from the apices of the new pseudo-bulbs; one foot long and drooping. Flowers, small, pinkish-white, closely set on the raceme and distinctly "cupped" (hence the specific name).

PLATYCLINIS

A small genus of tropical epiphytal orchids from New Guinea and Philippine Islands.

They may be grown in pots or baskets in a well-drained compost and require plenty of warmth and moisture during the growing season with a long rest afterwards.

P. filiformis.

Pseudo-bulbs, oblong-ovate, one inch high, bearing two apical, grassy leaves four inches long. Raceme, many-flowered, arching, produced in summer from the apices of the new pseudobulbs.

Flowers, small, very fragrant, pale yellow-green. It is sometimes known as *Dendrochilum filiformis*.

PLEIONE

A small family of tuberous-rooted, epiphytal, deciduous-leaved orchids, natives of India, etc. They are of easy culture and are a great attraction when in flower, but are not suitable to low elevations.

They are suited to pot culture and enjoy an open, well-drained compost. During the growing season they should be liberally treated as regards water but when the flowers and leaves have fallen they should be rested for a considerable time in a dry and airy position. They should again be potted up in the spring, taking care that the tubers are not deeply bedded in the compost. Water should be supplied very carefully and sparingly until the new growths are well established and growing vigorously.

P. Hookeriana.

Native of India; has large, rosy-mauve flowers, slightly blotched with brown, and has a yellow throat. This species is well suited to a cool climate.

P. lagenaria.

Another Indian orchid, remarkable for its very handsome lip which is white, freely marked with purple, red, and yellow. This enjoys a slightly warmer position.

Others include:—*P. humilis, P. maculata, P. præcox.* The flowers in this genus are borne on upright stalks and much resemble crocuses in habit.

PODOCHILUS

A small family of epiphytal Asiatic orchids, requiring similar treatment to *Acriopsis.*

They are non-pseudo-bulbous and evergreen.

P. falcatus.

Native of Ceylon (4,000 feet). Stems four to ten inches long, flattened, clothed with small deep and green leaves, forming serrated edges. Flowers in a terminal raceme, four inches long and many-flowered; borne in summer. They are small, pale purple, heath-like.

RENANTHERA

A large family of tropical epiphytal orchids, natives of the old world, showy, and well worth cultivating.

They are very similar in growth, habit, etc., to *Arachnanthes*, but may be either climbing or tufted and compact. They enjoy a warm, moist climate and need not be severely rested.

The climbing species may be grown on posts and trellises or up trees, while the compact growing kinds (as *R. Imschootiana*) may be grown in an ordinary compost in hanging baskets.

Flowers usually showy and long-lasting. If the stems be allowed to fall over naturally, shoots will 'break' all along and many more flowers obtained.

R. arachnites.

A climbing species from Java. Stems fifteen to twenty feet high, clothed with two rows of stiff, ovate leaves.

Roots are produced freely from all parts of the stem and it is by these that it clings on its "host." Flowers produced at different seasons on long stiff racemes from the axils of the leaves. They are fairly large and "spidery," brownish-yellow, blotched, and spotted with purple.

R. Imschootiana.

A dwarf, slow-growing, compact plant, native of Burma. Stems thick and woody, one foot high, bearing four or more dark green, tongue-shaped, leathery leaves. Flowers are borne on a drooping axillary raceme. They are bright red and yellow, some two and a half inches across. Lip, small, deep crimson with a white blotch in the throat.

R. Maingayi.

A climbing, large-growing species from Java, very similar in growth and habit to *R. arachnites*. Flowers are borne on a long, arching and branched raceme, many feet in length, in spring and summer.

They are large, and very much resemble a scorpion in shape; lilac, spotted and blotched with purple. Lip, small, yellowish; a very showy orchid, and very variable as to colour.

Other species include;—*R. coccinea*, *R. Storeii*, etc.

RHYNCOSTYLIS

A small family of epiphytal, tropical, Asiatic orchids, requiring similar treatment to Aerides.

There are about three species in cultivation and these are often known as *Saccolabiums* (which they much resemble in habit, growth, etc.).

R. cœlestis.

Leaves, thick and fleshy, channelled, bilobed at the apex, produced fanwise.

Raceme, drooping, many-flowered, produced at different seasons. Flowers, small, white and blue.

R. retusa. (*Saccolabium Blumei*, *S. guttatum*, etc.).

The 'fox-brush' orchid, native of Ceylon (dry zone) and India. Leaves, one foot or more long, stiff and fleshy, channelled, and unequally bilobed at the apex, produced fanwise from the erect stem.

Raceme, pendent and many-flowered, produced in spring and summer. The flowers are individually small but are produced in great quantity. They are fragrant and long-lasting, white, dotted with rosy-pink. There are several minor varieties of this species, the white one being very beautiful.

RODRIGUEZIA

A small genus of epiphytal South American orchids; they are not difficult to grow and are best accommodated in baskets.

The pseudo-bulbs should be made firm on small pieces of tree-fern or bark and the only compost required is broken crocks, charcoal and moss. They need plenty of water during the growing season, and must never be severely rested.

They are, however, not common in cultivation.

R. fragrans.

A beautiful species from Brazil. Pseudo-bulbs small, rounded and flattened, bearing two apical, leathery leaves, five inches long and stiff. Scape erect, produced in summer from the base of the mature pseudo-bulbs.

Flowers, large, pure white and very fragrant. The lip has a yellow blotch in the throat.

Other species include:—*R. candida, R. decora*, etc.

SACCOLABIUM

A large family of tropical, epiphytal orchids, natives of Asia.

They require basket treatment in an ordinary compost and enjoy plenty of light and moisture in a warm position during the growing season with a decided rest when growth is complete.

Flowers usually borne on a many-flowered raceme; they are usually small, but are produced in great profusion and are fragrant and showy.

S. ampullaceum.

Native of India. Leaves, short and fleshy, channelled, and bilobed at the apex, borne in two rows on the short, erect stem.

The erect axillary raceme is short and crowded with purplish-rose flowers and is borne in autumn.

S. bellinum.

Native of Burma. Stems, semi-erect; leaves produced in two rows, thick, eight inches long, strap-shaped, deeply channelled and bilobed at the apex. The axillary racemes are stiff and bear about six flowers in spring. The flowers are produced in a cluster and are nearly two inches in diameter. They are deep olive colour, blotched with brown; the large lip is pure white and crisped, blotched centrally with yellow, and has a slight spotting of purple.

S. bigibbum.

A rather scarce species from Upper Burma, which has not yet flowered in my collection. Leaves thick, short, and leathery, narrow and recurved.

The erect flower-spikes carry from three to five yellow and white flowers.

S. Blumei.

(*Rhyncostylis retusa*).

S. cœleste.

(*Rhyncostylis cœlestis*).

S. curvifolium.

A pretty little species from Burma, Java, etc. Stems, one foot or more high, erect, clothed with two rows of recurved, channelled leaves, which are narrow and stiff and about six inches long. Raceme, erect, many-flowered, produced in winter and spring. Flowers, medium-sized, bright vermilion. The bracts are bright purple.

S. guttatum.

(*Rhyncostylis retusa*).

Other species include:—*S. Huttoni*, *S. giganteum*, etc.

SATYRIUM

A small family of terrestrial orchids. They require pot treatment and are of easy culture if treated as advised for *Ipsea.*

S. Nepalense.

A native of Ceylon (5,000 feet) and Northern India. Bulbous-rooted. Leaves, ovate, acute-pointed, pale green.

Spike, erect, six to ten inches high, clothed with small fragrant pink flowers; borne in spring.

SCUTICARIA

A small family of curious terete-leafed epiphytes from tropical South America.

They are best grown on blocks of tree-fern with a little moss tied about the roots and suspended where they can obtain plenty of light and moisture.

S. Hadwenni.

Leaves, ten to twelve inches long, cylindrical. Flowers borne on drooping scapes. They are some two inches across, pale yellowish-green, blotched with chesnut brown.

The comparatively large lip is white, margined with pale purple and irregularly blotched with brown. Another is *S. Steelii.*

SELENEPEDIUM

A fairly large family of terrestrial or epiphytic orchids from South America.

They are nearly allied to *Cyprepedium* and require the same treatment. Habit, growth, etc., is similar to *Cyprepedium.*

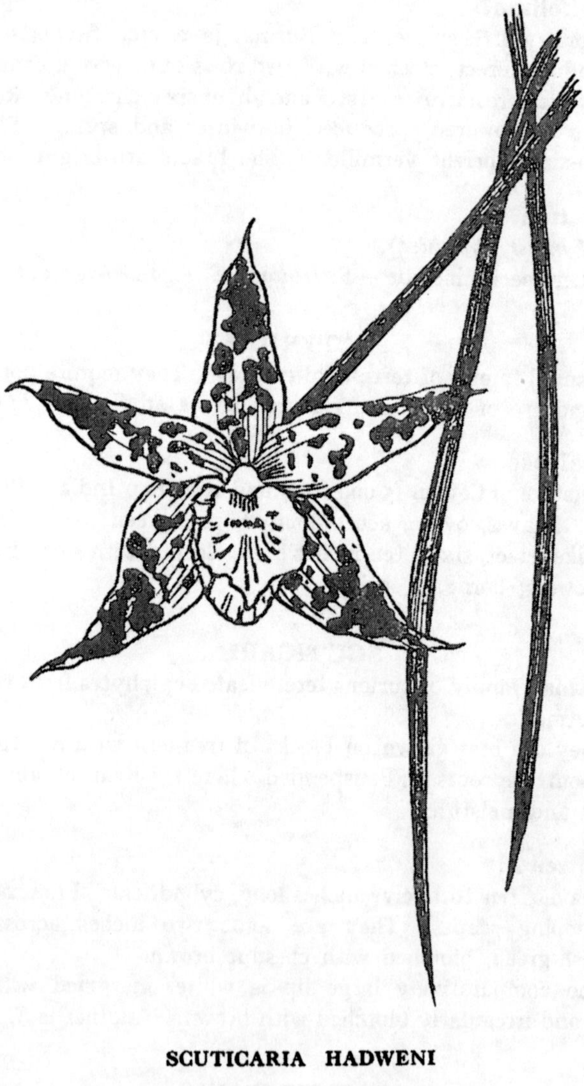

SCUTICARIA HADWENI

S. calurum.

This is a fine hybrid between *S. longifolium* and *S. Sedenii*. Leaves ten inches long, strap-shaped, acute-pointed, glossy green.

Scape, erect, two to three feet high, bearing six or eight large flowers, which are brownish yellow, shaded with white. Petals, long and narrow, twisted, green, white and pink, pouch small, pale green, shaded with brown.

S. cardinale.

This is a hybrid between *S. Sedenii* and *S. Schlimii albiflorum*. In habit, etc., very like the foregoing. Flowers produced freely on erect stems at different seasons. They are delicately shaded with rosy-purple and green on a white ground. Pouch, medium size, white, shaded with green and purple.

S. Sedenii.

This is a hybrid derived from *S. Schlimii* and *S. longifolium*. Similar in habit, growth, etc., to the foregoing.

All the above require plenty of water during the growing season and should not be severely rested. They are admirably suited to growing at the higher elevations.

SOBRALIA

A fairly large family of terrestrial tropical orchids, natives of South America. They are easy to grow, but are not widely cultivated. This is perhaps because the large and showy flowers are of short duration and are consequently of no value for cut flower purposes or for decorations, although a succession of flowers is produced from one spike.

They require a light, moist position and enjoy plenty of water when in full growth, but though they need less when this is complete, they should never be allowed to get dry.

S. macrantha.

Is the species oftenest met with. It has reedy stems, very similar to *Arundina bambusifolia*, but taller, some three to five feet high.

Leaves, lanceolate, acute-pointed, grassy.

SOBRALIA (Hybrid)

The flowers are borne in succession from the tops of the leafy stems. They are large and very showy, very similar to *Cattleyas* in form and coloration. They are some six inches or more in diameter and of a deep purple throughout. The lip has a blotch of lemon yellow. They last about two days in full beauty, but this is somewhat compensated for in the fact that several flowers are borne in succession.

S. Xantholeuca.

A magnificent species which bears a succession of very large bluish-white flowers from April to July. The large, spreading lip is stained with yellow and pale rose and is deeply 'crested.' This species seems more amenable to cultivation than several of the others, and is always handsome, even when not in bloom.

Other beautiful, but scarce species include:—*S. Lowii, S. sessilis,* etc.

SOPHRONITIS

A small family of epiphytal orchids from the mountainous parts of South America.

They are easy to cultivate at the higher elevations (4,000 to 6,000 feet) if kept damp and shaded. They will not succeed at lower elevations.

They require to be cultivated in baskets of moss with plenty of moisture at all times.

S. grandiflora.

This is the most well-known and showy species. Pseudo-bulbs and leaves similar to a minute *Cattleya.* They are one inch high, swollen, one-leafed and very crowded. The leaves are oval and leathery. The flowers, which are large for the size of the plant—being some three inches across—are borne singly on an erect stem from the apices of the mature pseudo-bulbs in winter.

They are of a brilliant scarlet, while the deep yellow lip is streaked with the same colour.

This family has often been crossed with *Cattleyas, Brassavolas* and *Lælias,* but the offspring are all moderately 'cool-growers.' Many are exceedingly beautiful and well worth growing at the higher elevations.

SOPHRO-CATTLEYA

A growing family of hybrids derived from inter-crossing *Sophronitis* and *Cattleya*. They may be treated as advised for *Cattleyas* and are well worth cultivating for their (usually brilliant) flowers.

SOPHRO-CATT-LÆLIA

A tri-generic family obtained by inter-crossing *Sophronitis, Cattleya* and *Lælia*. They are interesting, often beautiful; easy to grow, being treated as *Cattleyas*.

SPATHOGLOTTIS

A fairly large family of terrestrial orchids which are very showy when in flower. They need a good open and well-drained compost in which the tubers should be just buried. During the growing season they enjoy liberal waterings but when this is complete they should be kept fairly dry for some time in order to induce the flowers to appear. This genus includes the common 'ground orchid' which finds a place in practically every Colombo garden.

S. Vieillardi.

A native of New Caledonia. Leaves two feet long by three inches wide, acute-pointed and 'ribbed.' The flower-spike is produced in late summer from the bases of the leaves; it is some three feet high, erect and many-flowered. The flowers are about two and a half inches in diameter and of a beautiful rosy-lilac colour. Lip, large, trilobed. The flowers are very long-lasting.

Others include:—*S. aurea, S. Fortunei,* and there are many beautiful garden hybrids.

STANHOPEA

A fairly large family of very showy-flowered, short-lived, large and exceedingly fragrant orchids, all of which are epiphytes.

They are natives of South America and are exceptionally showy when in full bloom; their structure being most peculiar.

They are of easy culture and blossom regularly with very little attention.

SPATHOGLOTTIS. AUREO-VIEILLARDII
(Variety) Slightly reduced

To face page 102

A remarkable feature of these orchids is their habit of producing the pendulous racemes from the bottoms of the mature pseudo-bulbs.

To provide for this, they should be cultivated in baskets, which have plenty of room to allow the racemes to push their way down through the compost. A few narrow pieces of wood laid about one inch apart will permit this and will be quite sufficient to keep the compost from washing or falling out.

They enjoy a light, warm, and moist position with plenty of water during the growing season, with a reduced supply and cooler conditions during the resting season, but should never be dried severely.

Whilst in bloom the flowers should not be allowed to come nto contact with any water, or they will fade at once.

S. bucephalus.

This is one of the best-known of the family and is easy to grow. Its pseudo-bulbs are oblong-ovate, deep green, furrowed when mature. The leathery leaves are fifteen inches long, stalked and broad, erect.

Raceme is borne in summer from the bases of the mature pseudo-bulbs, it is about eight inches long and bears about five very fragrant flowers.

The latter are about four inches in diameter and of a rich orange, blotched, and spotted with deep red; the column is white, shaded with green and spotted with deep purple. The large trilobed and curiously-shaped lip is orange-yellow dotted with purple.

S. oculata.

Pseudo-bulbs egg-shaped, two inches high, furrowed. Leaves, stalked, one foot high, 'ribbed.' The large and fragrant flowers are produced on a pendent scape, they are often five inches in diameter, and some four or five are borne. The flowers are pale yellow, spotted with purple, while the lip is white, thickly spotted with crimson and purple. A native of Mexico.

Other beautiful species include:—*S. insignis*, *S. tigrina*, *S. platyceras*, *S. graveolens*, etc.

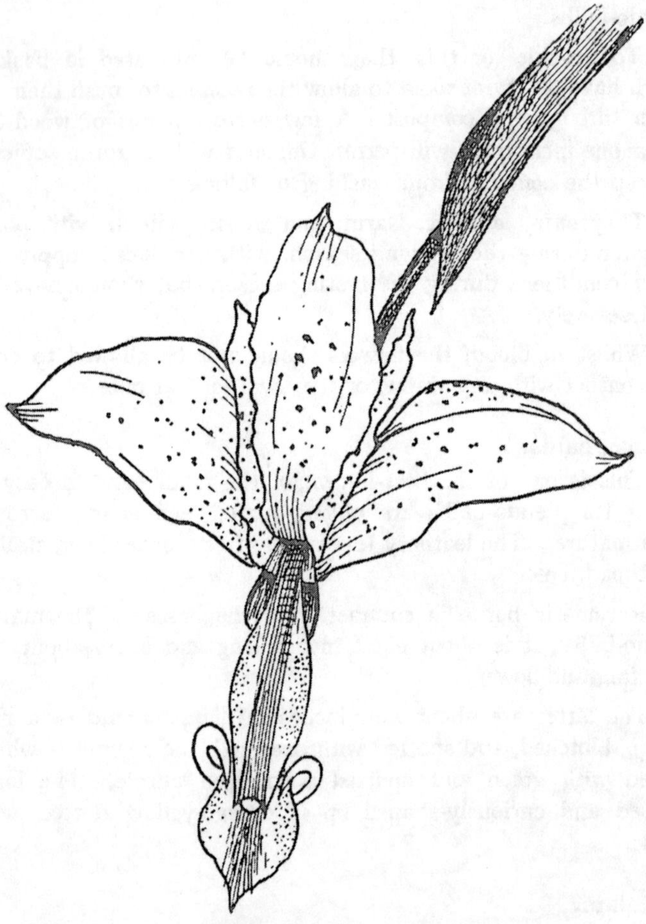

STANHOPEA GRAVEOLENS

STAUROPSIS

A small family of epiphytal tropical orchids, natives of India, Malaysia, etc. They are rather like *Vanda* in habit, and may successfully be cultivated under the conditions that are afforded to *Aerides* or *Vanda*. They enjoy plenty of heat and moisture if they are to flower well.

S. lissochiloides.

Native of Malacca. Stems, thick, erect, often five feet high bearing two rows of thick, recurved, leathery leaves, and a quantity of clinging, thick white roots. The spike is many-flowered and erect, borne in summer. The flowers are nearly three inches in diameter, deep yellow, spotted with reddish-brown; lip rosy-purple. This plant (and indeed the other members of the genus also) is inclined to flower well only when the plants have attained a fair size.

Another is:—*S. gigantea.*

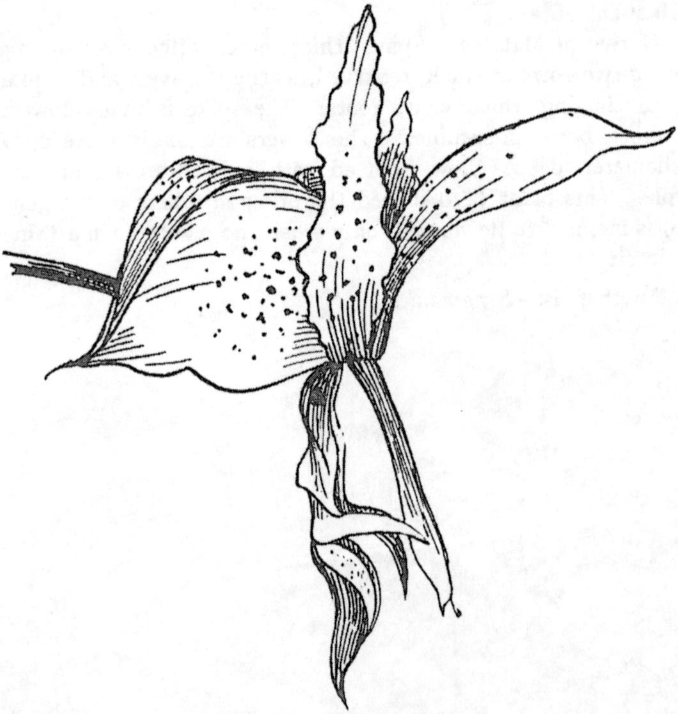

STANHOPEA GRAVEOLENS

TAINIA

A small genus of terrestrial epiphytal orchids, natives of Asia. They require pot-treatment with some decayed leaves in the compost and similar conditions to *Calanthes*.

T. bicornis.

A native of Ceylon (3,000 feet). Pseudo-bulbs, three inches high, swollen and fleshy, deep green, bearing one apical, stalked leaf, deeply nerved and broad.

Flower-scape erect, many-flowered, produced in summer from the base of the mature pseudo-bulbs, they are medium-sized, pale olive green stained with reddish-brown.

THUNIA

A small but very showy-flowered genus of (I believe epiphytal) tropical orchids, natives of Asia. They are non-pseudo-bulbous and produce annually a stout, erect and fleshy stem two to three feet high, pointed and bamboo-like. They are best cultivated in pots as for *Calanthes*, in a good open compost and they enjoy liberal waterings with a hot, moist climate during the growing season.

T. alba.

This is very similar to, but smaller than *T. Marshalliana;* thus a description of the latter will serve.

T. Bensoniæ.

A very handsome species from Burma and India. Stems erect, two feet high, bearing two rows of pale green, broad, and pointed leaves.

Flowers are borne in a cluster of five or more from the apices of the leafy stems in summer. They are some three inches across and of a rich rosy-purple; the large spreading lip being deep purple and crisped at the edge.

T. Marshalliana.

This is about the best of the family, and is an exceptionally showy and free-flowering orchid. Stems erect, three to four feet high, leaves similar to *T. Bensoniæ*. Flowers in a terminal cluster, borne on the tops of the leafy stems in summer. They are very large and graceful, some five inches or more in diameter.

They are star-shaped and of a pure glistening white. The large frilled and spreading lip is also white, but is veined with purple and has a blotch of yellow in the throat. The interior portion carries a quantity of golden-brown hairs.

These orchids produce stems which are of annual duration only, another springing up at the commencement of the growing season (about March). Consequently they must be given a prolonged rest when the leaves and flowers have dropped.

During the resting period they should be well ripened by exposure to sun and air, but when the new growths appear they should be potted up at once and watered sparingly until the growth has advanced; they may then be watered copiously and otherwise encouraged to grow freely. When the young growths are well established, the old stems may be cut off and cuttings taken as advised (see introduction).

As these plants are inclined to be top-heavy, they should be well fixed in the compost and given a supporting stake.

TRICHOSMA

The only member usually cultivated in this family is *T. suavis* (also known as *Eria coronaria*, which see). It is a native of Darjeeling.

THUNIA MARSHALLIANA

To face page 108

VANDA

An extensive genus of tropical epiphytal orchids, that are confined to the old world.

They are of easy culture and are well worth growing, being very floriferous and the flowers are usually showily coloured, fragrant and long-lasting.

They may be cultivated in pots, baskets, or fastened on to trees. They enjoy plenty of sunlight, warmth and moisture during the growing season (which is evidenced by the lengthening of the roots and the production of new foliage), but require a rest when this is complete.

As their roots are chiefly ærial, they require very little compost and a free passage of air about the roots is advantageous.

The following species are among the best (but there are many more in cultivation):—

V. Amesiana.

A compact, erect-growing dwarf species, native of Burma. Leaves ten inches long, erect, narrow, dull green and fleshy, channelled and acute-pointed.

Flowers borne on an erect, many-flowered raceme, some eighteen inches high, bearing a large number of white, pink-flushed flowers which are nearly two inches across. The lip is deep rosy-purple. Flowers, very fragrant and long-lasting.

V. Bensoni.

Stems erect, ten inches high, bearing two rows of leathery, bilobed leaves some eight inches long. Axillary raceme eighteen inches long, borne in summer. About a dozen flowers are produced, some two inches in diameter, sepals and petals greenish-yellow dotted with brown. Lip, large, white, rose, and purple.

V. Boxallii.

V. cærulea.

A favourite and very beautiful free-flowering orchid from Burma. It will succeed at all elevations and bears profusely at different seasons of the year, chiefly perhaps in autumn.

H

Stems erect, one foot or more high, bearing two rows of leathery strap-shaped, stiff and bilobed leaves.

Raceme strong and arching, bearing ten or more lovely pale-blue flowers. The latter are some three inches across. When they are first open they are pale and small, but soon expand and the colour becomes more pronounced. Lip, deep blue, stiff.

This is a really first class orchid and is very showy and free-flowering, the blooms remaining about two weeks in perfection. A plant in my collection has borne no less than four large racemes during the five months January to June.

This is, of course, too much, and is apt to weaken the plant; but is easily remedied by cutting off the racemes if they are produced too freely. This species does not require any great heat.

V. Kimballiana.

A very beautiful and free-flowering species from Burma. Stems, semi-erect, bearing purplish-green drooping leaves, which are very similar to those of *V. Amesiana*, but are not so stiff.

Roots are produced freely from all parts of the stem. The flowers are borne on a brownish-purple, stiff, many-flowered raceme, which emerges from the axils of the leaves in summer and autumn.

They are some two inches across. Sepals and petals pure white; lip, large and spreading, crisped at the margin and elongated into a spur at the back.

It is of a beautiful, rich purple with some orange on the sides and in the throat. Very fragrant.

V. Parishii.

Native of Burma. Stems short and sturdy—of slow growth. Leaves, thick and leathery, oblong, bilobed at the apex. The erect raceme bears about eight fairly large, fragrant flowers, which are greenish-yellow thickly spotted with brown. Lip, large, white, streaked with orange, and tinged with amethyst.

V. Roxburghii.

Native of Ceylon and India. Stems erect, leaves stiff, channelled and bilobed, eight inches long, narrow. Racemes, strong and many-flowered, axillary; produced in spring and summer.

SINGLE FLOWER OF VANDA SANDERIANA
(Natural Size)

To face page 111

The flowers are fragrant and long-lasting, two to three inches in diameter, yellowish-green, mottled with brown. The lip is trilobed, the front lobe being purple while the side lobes are white. Spur pale pink.

There are several varieties of this plant, which are rather scarce. One differs from the type in that the flowers are tinged with pink, while the front lobe of the lip is deep pink, and I have lately seen two more varieties, one bearing white and the other yellow flowers.

V. Sanderiana.

An exceedingly fine plant from the Philippines. The flowers are very large—often five inches or more in diameter. Stems, stiff, erect, bearing long leathery leaves. The raceme is produced from near the top of the stem in autumn, and bears three to five large flowers. They are very showy and long-lasting. Sepals and petals white and rosy-purple, tinged with saffron and spotted with red at the base (the lower sepals are beautifully netted with brown and have a tinge of grey on them). Lip, small, dull red and yellow. This is a rare plant and enjoys a hot, steamy position.

V. spathulata.

A showy-flowered, climbing species, native of Ceylon. Stems cylindrical, five to ten feet high; leaves, narrow, stiff, acute-pointed.

Raceme terminal, strong, arching and many-flowered, borne in autumn. Flowers one and a half inches across, scented, bright yellow.

V. teres.

A very beautiful orchid from India, Burma and the Straits.

It is of a climbing habit, three to six feet high. Stems, cylindrical, dark green, as thick as a quill. Leaves, similar, pointed, about five inches long. Roots are produced freely from all parts of the stem.

The stiff racemes are borne in summer and autumn from the top part of the stems and carry three to five large flowers.

The latter are nearly three inches in diameter, white, flushed with rose. The large trilobed lip is notched in front and coloured deep rose. The side lobes are white and form an arch over the orange-tinted and purple-veined throat.

This species enjoys all the sunlight it is possible to give it and must be given plenty of moisture in the growing season, with a decided rest when this is complete. There are numerous varieties of this species and it has been largely used by the hybridist.

V. tricolor.

An extremely handsome-growing and free-flowering orchid from Java.

Stems erect, one foot or more high. Leaves produced fan-wise, one foot long, recurved and channelled, bilobed and narrow; stiff.

Raceme, axillary; borne in early summer; stiff and many-flowered. The flowers are large and fragrant, yellow, spotted and blotched with brown; lip, bright purple with touches of orange. This species is very suitable for pot culture.

Other beautiful species include:—*V. cristata*, *V. Hookeriana* (which is very similar to *V. teres*), *V. suavis* (very similar to *V. tricolor*), etc.

VANILLA

A small family of epiphytal orchids, natives of Malaysia, Ceylon, etc. The plants are of a creeping (ascending) habit, and should be tied on to trees or branches under light shade. They are essentially plants that must be grown in a hot and moist position

V. planifolia.

This plant is remarkable in that it is the only orchid that produces a food product (the pods of this species being the vanilla of commerce). Stems, climbing, fleshy, and channelled. Leaves, oblong-ovate. Flowers, large and flat, dull yellow, rather lacking in interest.

Native of South America. Other species include:—*V. Walkeriana*.

ZYGOPETALUM

A very large family of epiphytes from tropical Central and South America.

They may be pseudo-bulbless or furnished with stout pseudo-bulbs.

They will succeed with the *Cattleyas*, but those without pseudo-bulbs should not be severely rested in any way, while they require more shade. The whole family is well worth representation in collections for the sake of their often peculiarly-coloured flowers.

The smaller species should be given a little open compost and be placed in small baskets, while the larger kinds can well be tied on to blocks of tree-fern root.

This genus is, I believe, but little known in Ceylon as yet, and I have only one member left.

Z. Wendlandii.

Without pseudo-bulbs. Leaves in a small tuft, pale green, six to nine inches high. The solitary flowers are borne in succession from April to July from stems which spring from the sheathing bases of the leaves. They are comparatively large, and fragrant. The sepals and petals are greenish-white, while the open, spreading lip bears a large central blotch of violet-blue. It is a handsome, long-lasting flower.

The following are pseudo-bulbless—*Z. Candidum*, *Z. cerinum*, *Z. cochleare*, and *Z. cœleste* as well as many others; while for the section with pseudo-bulbs may be taken the following—*Z. crinitum*, *Z. Gautieri*, *Z. grandiflorum* and *Z. maxillare*, all of which are very well worth a place.

ZYGOPETALUM WENDLANDII

SELECTION OF ORCHIDS FOR CULTURE AT DIFFERENT ELEVATIONS

As it may be of advantage to beginners to know which orchids are best suited to cultivation at the different elevations, I append a list of orchids that may safely be recommended to start a collection with, and for this purpose have divided them up as follows:—Low (sea level to 1,500 feet). Medium (1,500 feet to 3,500 feet) and High (3,500 feet and upwards). It must be remembered however, that orchids, in the same manner as many other plants, will often grow under conditions that are very different to those under which they naturally thrive; but they will only luxuriate when the artificial conditions most resemble those that obtain in their natural habitats; thus beginners would do well to cultivate those that are best suited to the climatic conditions that occur in their own districts, but when they become more accustomed to the culture of these plants there is no reason why they should not try their skill on plants that are of more difficult culture, and attempt to give them, artificially, their natural conditions.

It must also be clearly understood that there are very many more orchids then are here enumerated; many of which are showy and easily managed, but are not, so far as I am aware, yet in Ceylon collections.

Orchids Suited to Low Elevations

Acanthophippium
Acriopsis
Aerides
Ancistrochilus
Angræcum
Anguloa (*Clowesii*)
Anœctochilus
Arachnanthe
Arundina
Brassavola
Bulbophyllum Lobbii, Dearei
Calanthe (with the exception of *C. purpurea* and *C. veratrifolia*)
Catasetum

Cattleya (provided they can be kept out of the Monsoon rains)
Chysis
Cælogyne (except *C. corrugata, C. ocellata, C. odoratissima, C. elata,* and *C. lentiginosa*)
Cottonia
Cymbidium (except *C. ensifolium* and *C. eburneum*)
Cyprepedium (most of these seem to thrive at all elevations)
Dendrobium (except *D. aureum* and *D. Falconeri*)
Epidendrum
Eulophia
Geodorum
Gongora
Grammangis
Grammatophyllum
Habenaria
Liparis (longipes)
Oncidium Lanceanum, Luridum, Papilio
Peristeria
Phaius (except *P. bicolor*)
Phalænopsis
Pholidota
Platyclinis
Renanthera
Rhyncostylis
Saccolabium
Sobralia
Spathoglottis
Stanhopea
Stauropsis
Tainia
Thunia
Vanda
Vanilla

A selection for Medium elevations may include, in addition to most of the foregoing:—

Anguloa (in cool places)
Brassia
Brasso-Cattleya
Cattleya
Cirrhopetalum

Cœlogyne corrugata, C. elata, C. lentiginosa
Cycnoches
Cyperorchis
Dendrobium aureum (in cool places)
Epi-Cattleya
Epi-phronitis
Eria
Ipsea
Lælia
Lælio-Cattleya
Lycaste (in cool places)
Microstylis
Miltonia
Oncidium
Paphinia
Phaius bicolor
Podochilus
Rodriguezia
Selenepedium
Sophro-Cattleya
Sophro-Catt-Lælia

Selection for High Elevations

As most of the above low and medium elevation orchids can be grown in *sheltered positions* or in glazed houses and verandahs, I do not propose to enumerate them again, but the following may only be cultivated at the higher elevations.

Bletia
Calanthe purpurea and *C. veratrifolia*
Cirrhopetalum grandiflorum
Cœlogyne odoratissima and *C. Cristata*
Cryptostylis
Cymbidium ensifolium and *C. eburneum*
Liparis Wightiana
Odontoglossum
Pleione
Podochilus
Satyrium
Sophronitis
Trichosma

INDEX